# The Plan

# The Plan

**Have Sex *Tonight*
with a Gorgeous Woman
in 69 Easy Steps**

**Tony Clink**

CITADEL PRESS
Kensington Publishing Corp.
www.kensingtonbooks.com

CITADEL PRESS BOOKS are published by

Kensington Publishing Corp.
850 Third Avenue
New York, NY 10022

All Kensington titles, imprints, and distributed lines are available at special quantity discounts for bulk purchases for sales promotions, premiums, fund-raising, educational, or institutional use. Special book excerpts or customized printings can also be created to fit specific needs. For details, write or phone the office of the Kensington special sales manager: Kensington Publishing Corp., 850 Third Avenue, New York, NY 10022, attn: Special Sales Department; phone 1-800-221-2647.

First printing: October 2008

10  9  8  7  6  5  4  3  2  1

Printed in the United States of America

Library of Congress Control Number: 2008929364

ISBN-13: 978-0-8065-2886-1
ISBN-10: 0-8065-2886-9

# Contents

## The 69 Steps

# Introduction

Hi, I'm Tony Clink. You may not know me, but there are hundreds of thousands of people who do. For more than ten years, I have been one of the world's best-known chroniclers of the PUA (pick-up artist) underground. Neil Strauss, author of the worldwide bestseller *The Game*, acknowledges me as the person who inspired him to write about the world of men who dedicate their lives to picking up and sleeping with beautiful women.

My first book, *The Layguide*, is an encyclopedia of information on how to score with women, culled from more than ten years of research—both the exciting personal kind and the less exciting interviewing and web searching kind—and more than one hundred sources within the PUA community. It's been translated into nine languages and counting. It has been ranked in the top 5,000 on Amazon for more than three years, and was featured in a spread in Australian *Penthouse*.

I love that book. I think it's the best source of knowledge on women, men, and the interaction between them since Humphrey Bogart died. It's cool without being too cool and sarcastic without being annoying. It's occasionally even funny. But in the end it's still an encyclopedia of thousands of tips on everything from combing your hair to dropping an anchor by touching a girl's elbow. It's everything you'll ever need to create the you that you have always thought you wanted other people (especially women) to think you are. Complicated enough? I thought so.

I'm a teacher and a researcher. I'm a compiler of information. That's what I do. But I'm also a guy who has been with gorgeous women. I'm not particularly good looking; I'm not particularly smooth.

Call me a tender-hearted humanitarian, but I want to help men meet women and women meet the men of their dreams. And that man could very well be you. I want you to get out of the house, away from your obsessions, and into doing the only thing that is ever going to lead to happiness: talking to women. Thinking about it will never get you anything but a hairy palm. If you want it, you've got to act.

This time around, I'm taking a new approach: No more lectures. There's also another way of teaching, and that's leading by example. Remember that sex education class John Cleese taught in Monty Python's *The Meaning of Life*? The one where he brought in his wife and had sex with her right in front of the class? Well, that's going to be my approach.

*The Plan* is a deceptively simple concept. I'm going to walk you through the seduction of one beautiful woman, from walking into a bar to kissing her good-bye after a wild night of mutually satisfying sex. That's right, one encounter, but it's going to contain everything you need to know to go out and do it yourself. This is not the story of an actual experience; it's a composite of hundreds of experiences, pieced together into the perfect tool for teaching you how to play the game.

The structure of *The Plan* is not complex. I'm keeping it chronological, fast-paced, and straightforward. The sections are short. They focus on one very specific thing you should look for, do, and maybe most important, not do, while in the heat of the moment. I'd claim this book is the most fun you'll ever have, except most of you will finally go out and do the one thing in the world that's more fun within a few days of reading this book.

You've heard of the hands-on approach. This book is as hands-on as you can get..

# What You Will Learn from This Book

I'm sure you've heard this one before: A man walks into a bar.

In this case, that man is me—or more accurately, it's a character based on me that I've made up for this book. This character (me) is going to walk into a bar, looking for a woman. Not just any woman, a gorgeous woman who is going to end up in his bed by the end of the night.

In the next 69 steps, I'm going to walk you through exactly how to get from this moment—alone in a room full of strangers—to that intimate encounter with the woman of your dreams. I'm going to give you basic strategy. I'm going to show you how to move an encounter in the direction you want it to go. I'm going to teach you about psychology and the power of observation. I'm going to alert you to the obstacles (the blockers a typical girl will throw at you), and show you how to not only brush them aside, but turn them to your advantage. After reading this book, you will have every tool you will ever need to score with the woman of your dreams.

This book isn't about tricking women. It's about having the ability to make women think of you as their ideal man. It's about making them want, to practically beg, to have sex with you. And it's not going to happen just once. If you follow the advice in this book, it's going to happen all the time.

# How This Book Is Different

I've read thousands of pages of material on seduction. Much if it is wrong, and a lot of the advice isn't very helpful.

Why? Because it has no context. Read most books on seduction and you get a jumble of conflicting techniques, followed by stories that are more about bragging than giving good advice. Even if the techniques are sound, you aren't sure how to use them, when to use them, or which ones are most recommended. The websites are even worse. A beginner has no way of knowing which stuff is good, and which is not.

In this book, I've taken a different approach. Instead of giving you the whole grab bag, I've given you just the basic steps. Think of this as the sheet music for your personal concert, or the dance steps for your personal salsa.

At each step, I've chosen only the most recommended approaches, questions, conversational secrets, and closes. I've mostly avoided gimmicks; the gimmicks I have included are the ones I feel are the very best—the ones that get you to the next level with the least chance of making you look like a slimy, line-dropping amateur. You can feel confident that, if you use them correctly, they will work.

Even more important, I've put all of this advice in context. What did you do before this technique? What you are going to do afterward? What do you do if her response is positive? What if it is negative? What if you can't tell? I answer all these questions—and many more.

Basically, where everyone else gives you theory, I'm giving you the real thing, step by step. It's not up to you to choose which advice is best; it's not up to you to determine when to use these techniques and why. I've done all that work for you. All you have to do is follow the plan. That's why this is the easiest, most straightforward, and most useful seduction guide ever written.

# Why 69 Steps?

Yes, it's a gimmick. But it's also critically important to the central message of this book, which is this: Always remember why you are talking with this woman in the first place.

If your plan is to just be friends, get to know her, and have a nice conversation, well, more power to you, my friend. This book will definitely help you reach that goal.

I have a feeling though, that most of you have a different goal in mind. Let's call it a more physically oriented goal. No matter how good you're feeling about the conversation, it is critical to keep that goal in mind. Thus, each step here is leading you to . . . 69.* Yes, I know, 69 isn't your end goal, but I guarantee** that if you get to 69, there is no way you're not going the rest of the way.

---

*It has come to my attention that someone might not know what 69 refers to. If that person is you, don't worry, I'll explain. 69 is a sexual position in which a man and a woman face each other while lying in opposite but mutually advantageous directions (like a six and a nine, get it?) and perform simultaneous oral sex on each other. If you are thinking right now, *That's gross, I would never eat what a woman is offering,* well . . . you are decidedly in a minority. Get over it.

**This is not an actual guarantee, but you'd have to make a huge mistake, like not have the condoms handy, to screw up this encounter at 69. *Always* have a condom handy.

# How to Use This Book

If you are a beginner, you should follow the steps in this book exactly as they are laid out. Yes, I tell you exactly what to say to open the conversation. Yes, I tell you exactly how to invite her back to your place with no misunderstandings. Yes, this advice does work.

And yes, it takes practice to get everything right. You have to walk the walk, talk the talk, and understand that the woman sitting across from you is a human being with needs, desires, and hang-ups like everyone else. There's no way around it: you'll toss a few air balls before you start to hit your shots on a regular basis. When an air ball happens, go back to that point in the book and figure out what you did wrong. Do that a few times, and you will start to score . . . and score . . . and score.

Once you begin to have success on a regular basis (which you will), you will begin to develop a personal style. You will realize what works best for you and what you can't quite pull off, and you will become your own man. You start out as an apprentice; you work hard, and you eventually become a master. That's how life works.

No matter how much of a seduction master you become, this book will always be helpful. Consult it often to remind yourself of the basic rules of the game. Success will breed overconfidence, which will make you lazy. That's why professional baseball players take batting practice and watch tapes of their games: because no matter how good you are, you will hit a slump. And no matter how hot you are, you can always improve. Think of this book as seduction batting practice.

It doesn't matter what your goal is—you may want to have sex with a hundred gorgeous women, or you may be looking for a way to win over that one gorgeous woman in your school, office, or neighborhood—the advice in this book will work. It's time to make your dreams come true.

# The Plan

# Have the Right Attitude

Confidence is the most important trait to develop.
Confidence means you feel comfortable
approaching any woman, anytime, anywhere.

There are two components of the right attitude: being confident and having no fear of rejection. I'm going to go over both right now.

Confidence creates success; it is the most important trait you can develop. Confidence is your best friend and ally. Confidence means you feel comfortable approaching any woman at any time. Confidence means knowing this girl wants you to talk to her because you are the perfect man for her. She just doesn't know it yet.

Are you the perfect man for her? Of course. She will have more fun being with you than anything else she could possibly do in the next ten hours. It is a fact that most people are bored out of their mind. They keep looking around for someone else to make their boring lives more interesting. Well, you are going to be exactly the person to liven up her night and that's exactly why she'll be more than happy to meet you.

A successful man never wonders if he's good enough for a

woman; he wonders if the woman is good enough for him. Think this way: *I'm not trying to sell myself; I'm trying to find out what this woman has to offer.* Nobody wants to deal with a pushy salesman; you have to let the product (you) speak for itself. How? By talking about her. Project the focus onto the woman and you've already turned the tables in the game of seduction.

Don't worry if you try this new attitude and it doesn't work the first few times. Why? Because it's going to fail. A lot. Do you really expect to seduce every woman you talk to? Of course not. Wouldn't you be happy with half the women? Or even one in every three? Or one in every four?

The second key to being successful with women (or anything, really) is to be able to handle rejection. Don't let a bad experience get you flustered or destroy your confidence. Instead, think of rejection as a positive. Every time you get rejected, you learn something. Every time you fail, you're that much closer to being successful the next time. Take a cue from Thomas Alva Edison. Although it took him thousands of attempts to get the light bulb to work, he never viewed those unsuccessful attempts as failures. In fact, in his opinion, the thousands of tries that did *not* work only brought him closer to finding the solution that *would* work.

Did I say fail? Well shame on me, because there is no such thing as failure. In addition to bringing you that much closer to success the next time around, if a certain encounter doesn't end the way you'd like it to, then she's the one missing out. She's the one who failed your test, not the other way around.

# Forget About the Attitude

Now that you know about confidence . . . forget
completely that you've ever heard the word. If you
have to think about feeling confident, then you
probably aren't.

Now that you know about confidence . . . forget completely that you've ever heard the word. If you are thinking about feeling confident, then you're not really confident, you're nervous and unsure of yourself. Your goal is to be so positive about a sexual encounter that the word *confidence* never crosses your mind. Feeling so good and natural that you never have to think about confidence is the most confident act of all. Concentrate on feeling relaxed and positive, and you'll project an air of confidence every time.

If you've never felt that confident in life or when interacting with women, you'd probably have to start out by acting as if you do. As they say, "Fake it 'til you make it." If you're not confident, act as if you are. If you're not that funny, act as if you are. Sooner or later, you'll forget the act and switch to auto-pilot and before you know it—you are what you wanted to be without even trying!

If you need a little boost to approach a beautiful woman, do not tell yourself: "Be confident, be confident, be confident." Instead, repeat this mantra: "I am the best thing that has ever happened to this girl. I am the perfect experience for this girl." Now think of the goosebumps she will get because of the way you make her feel inside and if you're frisky, imagine for a split second all the ways you can make her cum. Don't dwell on it, though. Go and offer her the experience of a lifetime!

STEP **3**

# Look Good

**Never be afraid to ask a good-looking woman—
store employee, friend, stranger—for advice on
clothing and style. And the better looking that
woman is, the better.**

There's one in every crowd. The guy who thinks to himself: *But
I'm ugly. No woman will want to have anything to do with me.*

First of all, you're not ugly. Ugly is a state of mind, and a
state of mind can be changed. The more confident you are, the
better looking you become. Really, it's true, because the way you
carry yourself—the way you walk, talk, smile, and style—is
more important than the shape of your nose or the size of your
chin. Every guy who slouches and looks at the floor is ugly;
every confident guy looks good.

Okay, okay, some guys are ugly. Really ugly. It happens; life's
not fair. If you happen to fall into this very small percentage of
people (maybe 1 in 1000, so unless you are the ugliest person you
have ever known, this is not you!), don't worry, looks are only a
small part of the equation. Women care a lot more about how you
make them feel than how you look, so never use your looks as an
excuse not to approach any girl you want. Ever. I mean it.

You wouldn't believe how many good-looking guys are unable to get dates, let alone have sex with a woman. "How come?" you may wonder. Certainly good looks will grant the pretty boys a bit more initial attention from the ladies, but if they are unable to *hold* that attention, they will be dismissed in a hearbeat (and don't worry about how to do that, it'll be discussed later in this book).

But while your looks may not matter, your clothes certainly do. Designer names and an expensive look is one way to up your ratings, but you don't even have to be the best-dressed guy in the room as long as you are dressed smart. Ask a friend who you know is successful with the ladies to accompany you to a store to help you trade up your wardrobe. Better yet, ask a stylish woman to come along with you and give you advice—women love to give style advice.

If you're a novice to the clothing game, don't go trendy or over the top. Keep your look simple, classic, and elegant. Let your personality do the talking, but always appear clean and pressed. If you want to have a personal style, always go for the expensive look. There is no downside to looking well dressed, well groomed, and well off.

Notice I said expensive look, not expensive clothes. If you have the right person (usually a woman) to advise you, you can go to a second-hand store and walk out fifty dollars later with an absolutely stunning rack of expensive looking and stylish clothes.

As a last-ditch effort, you can hire an image consultant—some may be available for hire for double digits and some may even be available for free, courtesy of the department store.

Never be afraid to ask a good-looking woman—store employee, friend, stranger—for advice on clothing and style. And the better looking that woman is, the better. Remember: Every situation is a seduction situation and "its always on."

The last word on clothing: Always be comfortable in your skin. If the clothes you are wearing make you self-conscious or embarrassed, then they aren't the right clothes for you.

STEP **4**

# Always Be Prepared

> Before you head out that door, remind yourself
> that you are about to meet a beautiful woman—at
> the grocery store, at work, crossing the street,
> *everywhere*—and be prepared to do something
> more than stare at her rack or behind while hoping
> not to get caught.

The Cub Scouts have it right: Always be prepared. With that attitude, those guys must be chick magnets.

Meanwhile, if you've been to a club, you've seen those guys standing or sitting on the side of the dance floor, looking at the girls but not making a move, waiting for something to happen. Their mindset is, "If I stand around long enough, maybe a girl will notice me." What a sad bunch. That herd is known as death row, and I don't have to tell you that death row is not the place you want to be.

So why are *you* standing there on death row like someone waiting to be executed? I'm not talking about the night club; I'm talking about everyday life. Are you even noticing all those beautiful women you pass every day? Are you making eye contact? Are you saying, "Hi"? Are you trying to do something more than stare at their bodies when they're not looking and looking away as soon as they glance in your direction?

Some guys call this being oblivious, some guys call it being scared, but either way, you're on death row. If you're not taking advantage of the fact that you are surrounded every minute of the day by beautiful women, then you're no better than those chumps alongside the dance floor. Like them, you're going home alone, remembering all the beautiful girls you saw, and sleeping with your hand.

If you're in a club, the obvious answer is to hit the dance floor, bar, or chill-out areas and engage, engage, engage. Nothing's gonna happen unless you make it happen. The same is true in everyday life. Before you head out that door, remind yourself that you are about to meet a beautiful woman—at the grocery store, at work, crossing the street, *everywhere*—and be prepared to do something more than stare at her ass while hoping you don't get caught.

# Be in the Right Place at the Right Time

A bar is the worst place to pick up a woman. You're much better off trying to pick up a woman at the library or the coffee shop or just walking past her on the street. If you're a Cub Scout— always prepared—you'll find your success ratio is two to three times higher in the coffee shop than it is in the bar on Friday night.

Now that you're prepared to meet women, let's go out to the local bar and try to meet some.

But before we walk out that door, let me make a disclaimer: This book presents a scenario. It is set in a bar because that is the easiest place for the average man to understand. After all, bars are full of women. These women may have lowered inhibitions, and at least some of them are probably looking for a man. Plus, everything I have to teach you about picking up a woman in a bar can be used in any other situation where seduction takes place.

But remember this: A bar is the worst place to pick up a

woman. You're much better off trying to pick up a woman at the library or the coffee shop or just walking past her on the street. If you're a Cub Scout—always prepared—you'll find your success ratio is two to three times higher in the coffee shop than it is in the bar on Friday night.

Why? Because women in bars expect to be hit on by men. They therefore have their bitch shields up, ready to deflect unwanted advances. It is not because they are bitches inside—it is just that they get hit on in bars all the time and in the end it becomes physically impossible for them to be nice and kind and gentle to the umpteenth guy who comes to talk to them. It is nice to get noticed but too much of a good thing is never a good thing. So if you decide to go and fight an uphill battle in a bar environment, just keep in mind that it's nothing personal if a woman shoots you down.

In contrast, just think how a woman feels when you stop her on the street and start talking to her. She's not ready to be hit on, so her guard is down. She's going to assume you don't stop women on the street all the time. She's going to assume you really think she's special. In other words, she's going to be flattered.

There's one other thing to notice before we jump into this scene: You're alone. I know, alone is intimidating. Nobody wants to go into a bar alone. It's embarrassing. It's so much easier to have a buddy there to talk to during the down moments.

Exactly! You don't want a buddy there because it gives you an excuse not to approach women. When you're alone, you don't have much choice. You're either going to sit there like a chump staring into your beer, or you're going to get off your ass and talk to women. You want to give yourself every reason to overcome your fear and approach the woman of your dreams. So don't have a buddy there holding you back.

Plus, do you really want your buddy there to see you crash and burn? No. Trying to impress your friends with a smooth pick-up is the worst thing an inexperienced or slightly experienced ladies' man can do. It's too distracting, it's too much pressure, and it puts the woman on her guard. Most women don't want to be the hot slut you're high-fiving your friends about the next day.

An alternative method of arrival is to walk in like a rock star, surrounded by hot women (whom you've made friends with so they'll pimp for you, put in a good word, give social proof and make the other women jealous), greeted by bouncers, and welcomed by the manager. You will instantly be intriguing and interesting to all the women who are bound to notice your arrival, but this method's really meant for a more advanced stage of the game. By following the advice in the book you will eventually get there, but assuming that right now your choices are either to go alone or with a buddy, then its preferable to go alone.

So let's start again: A man walks into a bar. That man is me. I'm there alone, and I'm there to pick up a gorgeous woman. I'm also there to teach by example, so let's get started. . . .

STEP **6**

# The Invisible Panty Rule

There's a very important rule in seduction called
The Three Second Rule. Worship it. The rule states
that when you enter a seduction scenario, you
have three seconds, and only three seconds, to
make your move.

The first thing I notice when I walk in is that there are several
women in the bar and quite a few empty seats. There's a group
of guys in the corner. Hmm, they've got that office studs look;
could be competition. Three women are talking together at one
end of the bar. Two of them are pretty hot. Are they sisters or just
friends? How old are they? Then there's a woman sitting alone.
Why is that? Is her boyfriend in the bathroom? Then there's another hot woman . . . wait, did the second woman just glance at
me and smile? Or was she looking at her watch? She did it again.
What does that mean?

Whoa. Stop. Turn around. Start again, because this is never
going to work. That's what an AFC (an average frustrated, complaining, life-going-nowhere chump) would do. Seduction is

about trusting your instincts, not thinking yourself into a girl's pants.

I'm going to tell you something right now that's important, and that turns all the previous dumb-ass advice you've ever heard on its head: If you want to get laid, stop using your head on top and start using the one in the middle.

There's a very important rule in seduction called The Three Second Rule. Worship it. The rule states that when you enter a seduction scenario, you have three seconds, and only three seconds, to make your move. Well, you just spent fifteen seconds trying to outsmart yourself.

The thing to know when you walk into that bar is that you are going to approach a woman. You are not going to go sit at the bar, order a drink, and look around. You are not going to act like you're looking for a friend and walk around scoping the scene. You are not going to wait (and hope) that something happens. You are going to make a move in the first three seconds.

So forget the guys in the corner. They don't matter. Forget trying to figure out why the women are here and who they are with. Never make any assumptions. Assumptions will get you nowhere. The only way to find out about a woman is to talk to her.

There is only one question I ask when I walk into a bar: Which woman in here do I want to go home with tonight? I trust my instincts; this isn't a beauty contest. Don't stand there analyzing whether that butt is too wide or those breasts are too small. Go with your gut.

If you think a woman has noticed you, then that's probably the woman you should go after. Why? Because she probably did notice you, which means she's interested or at the very least, curious. Either way, she's putting out a vibe. She's open to being approached.

I call this The Invisible Panty Rule. There was something that drew you to that woman. Something, like a flash of panty, that made you stop. Your eye didn't see the panty, the open invite to seduction, but your mind did. It caught a signal. As you were scanning the room, something about her made you stop. That's your mind telling you she's the one. It's not telling you why; it's just telling you to go for it.

You know what that means for our man (me) who has just walked into a bar: two seconds in the door and I've made up my mind to approach woman #2. Right now, I can't tell you anything about her, with the possible exception of her hair color. I can't tell you the size of her nose, the cut of her dress, or the way she crosses her legs. I definitely haven't formed any half-baked assumptions about why she's here or what her personality is like.

But soon, if I play this right, I'll not just know what color panties she's wearing; I'll know what color everything else inside those panties is as well.

STEP **7**

# Eye Contact

Among all the pretense of the modern world, there is something very primal in a direct gaze. A mutual seduction can happen within seconds by just looking each other in the eye.

Most successful players can attest to the fact that creating and maintaining eye contact with a woman is the first key to success. Thrifty and shifty eyes signal insecurity, whereas a steady gaze signals confidence and creates attraction.

Some people find it absolutely impossible to look another person in the eye. If you're one of those people, fix that problem right now. Not looking people in the eye speaks of deep subconscious insecurities or deficiencies. It suggests you're trying to hide something, and you're afraid your eyes will give you away. Whatever those secrets and insecurities, real or imagined, the woman will pick up on them and try to remain at a distance.

On the other hand, once you're confident enough to keep your head up and your eyes wide open a seduction can happen with only a stare. Among all the pretense of the modern world, there is something very primal in a direct gaze. A mutual seduction can happen within seconds by just looking each other in the eye. If you catch a woman glancing at you, it is most definitely on. It is always on anyway, but now it is more on than ever. If she backs down, meaning she looks away, don't panic. Many guys fall for the look away, thinking, "Oh, she was just looking around and looked at me accidentally. It means nothing." Hey, puffball, what are you trying to do? Talk yourself out of sex?

It's not the look away that matters most; it's the glance back. If she glances back at you after initial eye contact, then that's it. She wants you and you want to be locked on to her eyes when that happens, not scanning the room for other people. By the way, the advice here applies to looking from across the room but even more important, to when you've already approached and are talking to a woman. Too often guys do just fine looking in a woman's eyes from across the room but once they get closer, they do anything but the thing that would grant them the most success.

To make a good initial impression it is important to pass the first test. If the girl doesn't look away immediately, you *fail* by looking away first. The woman is now thinking, "Yeah, he looked kind of interesting, but since he looked away, he is timid/insecure/has a low self-esteem/has something to hide . . . and I want nothing to do with him." But after that it is also important not to forget eye contact. Steady eye contact can convey and achieve a lot more than even the best of chatting, so remember—eye contact is one of the keys to a successful pickup.

---

### How to Hold Eye Contact

When you are talking to a woman, always maintain eye contact. This demonstrates confidence and intent. Yes, this means stare into her eye. Notice I said *eye*, not *eyes*. Don't glance from eye to eye; that makes you look nervous because your eyeballs will be moving back and forth like you're watching a tennis match. Pick one eye and stick with it.

STEP **8**

# Walk the Walk

If you want to impress women, you've got to learn to move like Neo . . .

Let's talk about body movement. If you've seen any action movies, you know slow is cool. Way cool. The coolest scenes in most movies are the slow-motion action sequences; they can induce goose bumps even during the lamest of movies. Well, guess what? You can induce goose bumps in women the same way! Women are drawn to men who seem to move and talk slower, as if they're bending time. Slow doesn't mean lazy; it means calm and deliberate.

A good place to start is to imagine you're moving like Neo (from *The Matrix*) during bullet-time sequences—move slower, blink slower, look in different directions slower, while still maintaining calmness and precision of movement. When you walk, walk slowly and gracefully. You may be tempted to run and fuss around a lot to suggest you're real busy and popular, but we all know the truly popular guys sit back and let the others come to them. Hopping from place to place like a rabbit suggests nervousness, which is not attractive at all. Walk calmly and confidently, like you have all the time and not a single care in the world.

For the best posture, keep your chest lifted and shoulders back, and pull in your stomach, making your body more attractive to women. It may be hard at first, but keep trying and sooner or later you'll find a posture you can maintain with minimum effort and maximum effectiveness.

Okay, major screwup alert here. If you are too conscious of your walk and posture, you are going to look like a complete moron. No woman will ever talk to a guy who's obviously puffing out his chest and walking like he's got a pinecone in his ass. It's even worse if he looks like he's walking in slow motion like Frankenstein. If you're going to pull this off, my friends, you need to practice.

Stand in front of the mirror at home. I know, I know, staring at yourself in the mirror is pretty lame, but this is important. Now relax and look at yourself with a critical eye. Do you have good posture? What do you need to do to improve it? Now walk like that . . . all the time.

The fact is this: You don't want to have to act differently in a seduction situation. You want your natural way of being to send the right message all the time. So get out there and walk like the confident, calm, and cool man you are.

# Talk the Talk

. . . and talk like Agent Smith.

It sounds like bullshit, but it's true: a deep rumbling bass voice is enough to get almost any woman wet. You could be a bald fat midget in a wheelchair, but if you talk like James Earl Jones you could still get almost any woman.

Unfortunately, most of us do not have sexy voices. Even more unfortunately, most of us make very little use of the mediocre voices we do have. You may have tried deepening your voice a few times and then reverted back to good old nasal. Well, that's not enough. Studies have shown that men deepen their voices subconsciously when speaking to attractive members of the opposite sex; you need to start doing it consciously and *all the time*. (Yes, even when talking to Grandma.)

First, all habits are hard to break, even good ones, so if you talk sexy to Grandma, you're going to talk sexy to the hot vixen at the coffee shop as well. Second, your voice does eventually deepen when you keep deepening it consciously.

So how to go about it? To deepen your voice, speak from your chest and your stomach, not your nose and your mouth. Put your hand on your chest and try to speak in a manner that allows you to feel maximum vibration emanating from your chest. Every time you notice you're no longer speaking from your chest and your stomach, start doing it again.

As for the manner of speaking, speak more slowly and deeper than you usually do, and use deliberate pauses. Try to overdo it at first (with Grandma, who probably has a hearing problem anyway) to get a feel for deep and slow.

Now that you walk like Neo, try talking like agent Smith—slow, cool, calm, precise, even to the point of being hypnotic. Don't worry about overdoing it. Once you get in an actual seduction scenario your adrenaline will speed you up just enough to kick you into the right gear.

# The First Words out of Your Mouth

The first words out of your mouth can make or break the conversation, so you'd better make them good. You're best off using a straightforward approach.

So here I am. I've got everything going right. I've entered the bar and used the Three Second Rule and the Invisible Panty Rule, which allowed me to follow my instincts in choosing the right girl immediately. I've tried to make eye contact (if I succeeded, good, if not, no biggie either), and I've walked up to her at a deliberate pace. She's sitting at the bar and apparently knows I'm coming, but she's looking away, not being flirtatious, so I have no idea what she's thinking of me.

And I don't care. I really don't. I gain nothing by trying to read her reactions right now. Maybe she looks nervous; maybe she looks ready to blow me off; maybe she looks excited but is trying to hide it. It doesn't matter. That's all in my mind—her thoughts haven't been revealed yet. I've already set my attitude to a positive, "this woman needs me" approach. My personality is what is truly going to influence her feelings about me now. What do I say?

The first words out of your mouth can make or break the conversation, so you'd better make them good. They have to be engaging, interesting, and hopefully will shift the focus from you to her for at least a moment so that while she answers, you can settle in and start to get a feel for her personality.

It's a little hot in the bar, so I order a drink, turn to her, and say: "So, it's kind of hot in here."

No. No. No. Bad idea. For one thing, that is a lame and pointless statement that simply shows you have nothing interesting to say. Second, it sounds like a pickup line. Third, it calls for a simple yes or no answer, a major mistake unless you're anticipating that answer and already have an open-ended follow-up question in mind. Lastly, you're focusing on a negative, making her think about something uncomfortable instead of something pleasant. You seem like a whiner, a major turn-off for women.

Instead, what you need to do is throw up a topic of conversation that will immediately get her talking and better yet, if she is with a girlfriend or girlfriends (which she probably is, since women seldom go to bars alone), will get them talking as well. And suddenly, you're the life of the party! So what do you do?

"Hey, I was just having an argument with a friend of mine and we just couldn't agree. So I'm thinking maybe I should get a female opinion on this. What do you think . . ." And now you ask the question that will get everyone talking.

Yeah, but what's the question? Let me put it in another way—what do women care about? What do women love more than anything? Cook up a question about anything that has to do with relationships, style, or looks, and always has a split opinion, and you'll get the conversation going. Just a few examples:

"What do you think, who cheat more, men or women?"—"Who lie more, men or women?"—"Who lie better, men or women?"— "Do blondes really have more fun? Why?"—"Should I dye my hair?"—"Do these clothes fit me? Should I try something different? What?"—etc., etc.

STEP **11**

# Touch Her . . . Immediately

> There's no way for me to find out a girl's attitude
> toward kino without giving it a try and pushing
> some limits, so I never miss an opportunity to
> touch her.

There is nothing sexier than touching. It is vital in any seduction scenario to touch the woman as much as possible without making her uncomfortable. We call this *kino* (short for *kinesthetics*, a fancy way of saying "making physical contact").

You'll learn to judge a woman's "kino-bility" as you gain experience. Some women love to be touched; in fact, some "kino girls" prefer touching to conversation. Other women hate to be touched, at least in public.

There's no way for me to find out a girl's attitude toward kino without giving it a try and pushing some limits, so I never miss an opportunity to touch her. And that first opportunity comes right now.

Any time I meet or am introduced to a girl, I shake her hand! This is an absolutely expected gesture, and a great source of first contact. I'm firm, but I don't squeeze, and always hold the handshake 3 to 4 seconds longer than expected while looking into her eyes. This makes her notice and think about the touch without creeping her out. I've invaded her personal space, but only barely and in an entirely appropriate way. I've also given her the impression that I'm powerful and direct—two very enticing attributes.

STEP **12**

# Ask Her Name?

Some argue that getting a name personalizes the
encounter. They say getting a name is like being
formally introduced. So what? Now you're just like
all the other guys who begin by asking for her
name and offering yours.

"Hi. I'm Tony. What's your name?"

Seems reasonable, right?

This may come as a surprise to you, but the answer is "No!"
Asking for her name might seem like an innocent and easy way
to start a conversation, but frankly this move is just plain lame.
Unless you are already of some value to her, why should she
even want to tell you her name? Maybe she doesn't want every
Joe to know her name. And unless you are already of some value
to her, why should she care to know your name?

So just as you shouldn't ask for her name, you shouldn't be
offering yours either. If she's not yet interested, she'll just forget
it. But if she's interested, she's going to ask for it. If in the middle
of a conversation, she suddenly says something like, "Oh my
gosh, I don't even know your name," that is a clear sign that
she's suddenly gotten interested in you.

Even better, you've taken a position of power. She's the one asking for your name. She's the one eager to get to know you better—in all the right ways. As you'll learn later, it's always better to have a woman give you her phone number or invite you over without you asking for it. This doesn't mean you have to be passive and wait for things to happen by themselves—believe me, they won't. But once you know how to coach her in the right direction and get her to ask all the right questions, you are a lot closer to your goals than if you were to ask those very same questions yourself. The same concept is at work here.

Some argue that getting a name personalizes the encounter. They say getting a name is like being formally introduced. So what? Now you're formally categorized as a chump or, even worse, *a friend*.

One more argument against asking for names: You ask for her name and then—you forget it! Now you're screwed, but not in the way you intended. If this happens, you've got to turn it back on her and make it seem like her name wasn't worth remembering. Try something like this, with a nonchalant, almost egotistical air, "I know you had a beautiful name . . . what was it exactly?" This may save your ass, but my question is, why did you set yourself up for this problem in the first place?

# The Opinion Opening

> Is it okay to use a standard opener on a lot of
> different women? Of course. You just have to be
> flexible enough to adapt it to each situation, and
> make sure it doesn't sound like a canned speech
> you give to all the girls.

There are a lot of conversation starters you can use to help you
through the awkward first few moments of an encounter. In my
first book, I listed almost ten that have worked repeatedly over
the years. But for the more practical approach of this book, I'll
give you my favorite one: the Opinion Approach.

Is it okay to use a standard opener on a lot of different
women? Of course. You just have to be flexible enough to adapt
it to each situation, and make sure it doesn't sound like a canned
speech you give all the girls. In fact, if you're a beginner, or lack-
ing a little confidence, I recommend starting out with just one or
two approaches for all your encounters. Not only will it save
you the trouble of trying to figure out which approach to use (resulting all too often in what's called "the paralysis of analysis"),
the practice will make you better at delivering the approach and

better prepared for the probable reactions—good, bad, and indifferent.

Always remember, though, both here and throughout the book, that the examples given are not mantras or magic combinations of words, the uttering of which will make all women fall into your arms. They're just examples, the effectiveness of which depends on how you are able to adapt them to the situation. Your job is not to memorize them word for word, then deliver them later to a mystified woman like a bad actor at summer stock. All too many guys make this simple mistake when just starting out, almost always resulting in a spectacular disaster.

Your job is to study these examples in order to understand their underlying dynamics. You need to understand what mental images are being used, and what kind of feelings they evoke in a woman.

Start off by memorizing the words, but realize you will outgrow them quickly. The approach that works best is the one you customize by applying the *principles* I'm about to explain here.

Let's step back into the bar. I've ordered a drink. Don't worry about your drink selection. It's not particularly important and anything goes as long as you can sip it without getting drunk. Remember, you've got a choice when you go to a bar: get drunk or get laid. It's very hard to do both unless you're looking to be one member of that last lonely drunk couple going home for a sloppy and forgettable hookup, so don't try it.

So I turn to the woman, make eye contact, and say, "Hey, can I ask for your opinion on something? I just had an argument with my friend today. He was saying I should change my style, that I'm not fully utilizing my potential the way I dress now. At first I said no way, but then I started thinking, maybe he's right. What do you think? I haven't really been paying much attention to what I wear as long as it's comfortable, but if you could give me a total makeover, what would you change? What would you add, what would you subtract?" Now shut up and listen. First, you are likely to get some good bits of information here that you'd better at least think about, if not act upon. But second, all of a sudden you are in conversation that should by all accounts be stimulating for the both of you. She'll be able to shine with her knowledge of style and fashion and feel as if she can make a difference in another person's life (and people generally do want to make a difference in other people's lives). And you'll be engaging in conversation with the woman you want to meet.

But no matter your approach, always remember to end the opener with an open-ended question. And yes, you must always avoid that old standby of the chump set, "Do you come here often?"

## Modification: This One Works, Too

Another one of my favorites is the Familiar Approach. In this case, you act like you know her—and that's it. Approach her like you'd approach any friend and act like you would with any good friend of yours. Ask her how she's been, what has she been up to in the meantime, what's going on in her life in the moment. After the initial surprise you'll probably get a "I'm sorry . . . do we know each other?" To which you can answer: "I'm sorry . . . don't we? You looked so familiar I was sure we were acquainted, but since I couldn't quite remember where I knew you from and I was too embarrassed to ask, I just thought I'd go with the flow and then maybe it would come to me during the course of the conversation. You know sometimes it happens that you meet a person you're sure you know, but you can't quite remember where from, so the only way to proceed is to talk to that person and then hopefully it'll come to you. So you're sure we haven't met someplace before?"

No matter what she anwers, I'm sure she'll be quite amused with the situation and since you're now talking anyway, it doesn't even matter that you didn't know her before, because now you do. Although I did caution against formal introductions above (like asking her name), this scenario can be the exception. Once you've established that you either really haven't met before or one of you simply doesn't remember the other one, it's quite safe to proceed with, "Okay then, since we're already talking anyway, why don't we get reacquainted? My name is . . ." Now give her your name and shake her hand as instructed above.

As always, it's important at this early stage not to seem like you are hitting on her, so be friendly (not fawning and drooling), be confident (not trembling and stuttering), and be humorous.

---

### Two Additional Options

- *The Fishing Trip.* You can fish to see if she thinks she looks like anyone famous by saying, "Do people often say that you look like someone famous?" Sometimes she'll respond with something like, "My friends say I look like Renée Zellweger." If that happens, it's a very good thing. Agree with her (even though you may not agree with her friends), mention something specific without being too complimentary ("It must be your eyes") and then move into a conversation about Renée Zellweger (or whomever she just mentioned).

- *The Pickup.* You end by saying, "You look exactly like . . . someone I should get to know better." This one's quite tame as far as pickup lines are concerned, but if this has you thinking in the direction of using pick-up lines in general, don't. Unless your delivery is convincing, women usually hate them, and they have horn-dog written all over them.

### How Was Your Day?

There's nothing more classic than walking up to a woman and asking about her day. This works best in a social situation, like a party at a friend's house, but it's equally good in any non-pickup (in other words, not a bar or club) environment. And of course, don't use this opener first thing in the morning. Wait at least until noon unless a long face is your desired response.

> **You:** "So, how was your day?"
> **Her:** "Great!"

Perfect. She's in a good mood, and since you're in a good mood she's going to feel some instant rapport with you. You smile and say, "So was mine. What did you do?"

But what if she says,

> **Her:** "Awful."

No problem. If her day was bad, she's going to want to talk about it, and that gives you the perfect opportunity to show that you're an empathetic, understanding guy who can make her feel wonderful, even on the worst of days. You put your hand on her shoulder and say, "I'm sorry. What happened?"

But what if she says,

> **Her:** "Okay, I guess."

This is a tougher cookie, but don't despair. Yes, she might be trying to brush you off or there's nothing in her day she wants to talk about. So you say, "Well then, what about yesterday?"

> **Her:** "It was fine."

Medic! We need fifty ccs of adrenaline over here STAT, this girl's about to fall into a coma. It's time for you to start creating some fun. If you can lift this girl out of the doldrums, you'll definitely be a whole lot closer to your goal. (And you do remember what that was, right?)

Raise your hands like you're measuring a fish about a foot long. "So you don't feel *this* excited?" She smirks, so you narrow your hands. "How about this excited?" Was that a slight muscle twitch? Is she starting to come around? Hold up one hand, thumb and finger an inch apart. "Could you possibly, at the least, be entertaining the thought of being *this* excited about life?" She smiles . . . and if you can bring a smile to the catatonic, she'll love you for it. If she still doesn't smile, oh well. It's good you found out this early and got away without having invested too much in her. Just excuse yourself. Even a completely random pick will probably yield you a more joyful companion.

# The Stunner Opening

> In general, telling a woman she looks stunning is
> not a very good approach, because it makes it
> seem like you're sucking up to her right off the
> bat. What most women are looking for instead is
> someone they can look up to. Therefore it's all in
> the delivery.

I picked this one up from the master of seduction, Ross Jeffries (www.speed-seduction.com). However, be warned that it's a pretty advanced technique. In general, telling a woman she looks stunning is the wrong approach, because it makes it seem like you're being a supplicating, overly horny chump who's only after her body. That's why, for this approach, it's all in the delivery. You have to talk slowly, radiating sincerity, confidence, and relaxed power. The key is to be low-key. If you come off horny or needy, this approach will never work.

Okay, I admit it; this is one of my favorite approaches. But I *never* use it in a bar or any other pickup situation. The Stunner Opening is used only *on the street*, when the woman is least expecting it.

It involves walking directly up to a woman, exuding power

but not rushing, and saying, "Excuse me (although you're really not excusing yourself for making her feel really, really good in just a few seconds), I just wanted to tell you . . . (pause to create anticipation) I think you're absolutely stunning, and I really want to meet you."

You've knocked her back on her heels, and she's going to take a moment to respond. Don't let her catch her breath. Immediately step forward *slightly* into her personal space and shake her hand. Now—and this is important—don't let go! Keep holding on as you continue to talk to her and look her directly in the eye. Some women may pull away and try to excuse themselves. If that happens, your delivery probably isn't quite there yet. This is a very obvious pickup but here's a secret: Most women *want* to be seduced. They *want* a mysterious stranger to approach them and they *want* to be swept off their feet. If you do this right, you will have made one of their fantasies come true within the very first minute of meeting you.

Now that she's stunned, you continue with "Actually I'm in a hurry, my friends/plane/limo/private jet is leaving in just a few minutes and I've really got to get going, but I'd really like for us to chat sometime and get to know each other better. Now how could we do that?" Notice that you didn't ask for her number, IM, or e-mail—you just created a situation in which she is bound to offer them to you herself. Unless of course she is still dazed by your approach and can only mumble, "Um . . . I dunno," in which case you "help her out" by saying: "Okay, listen, give me your number and I'll call you in the evening and then we'll talk."

Whether she likes you or not at this point is even irrelevant, because she's most likely going to give you her number anyway. First, because you are "in a hurry" and it is not polite to hold up people who are in a hurry. However you can't leave yet because you don't have her number, so in order to be polite and let you leave, she'll have to write down her number. Second, you are not a threat to her since you are obviously in a hurry to leave, but what harm could a phone call do and maybe you truly are a nice person to get to know, so why not. Third, she may simply still be too dazed from your unexpected approach and since she is unable to think rationally, she's just taking orders as they come.

A warning about using this approach on women who are truly stunning. They've heard it all before, so it's just going to sound like another come-on. Sure you can give it a try with the nines and tens as well, but they'll be a lot less stunned. The power of the Stunner Opening is in actually stunning the woman, or in other words, pleasantly surprising her. If she doesn't feel that her looks are stunning, or doesn't hear that kind of compliment often, you have a much better chance of success. A girl that is good looking but a little plain (the kind who grows on you the more you see her) is the perfect target for the stunner.

---

### One Last Opener Before We Go

I love this approach when I'm at Starbucks (or some other coffee spot), and it's amazing how well it works. If I see a good-looking woman sitting alone reading a book or working on her computer, I go up to her and say, "Do you mind if I sit here? There aren't any other seats." Then I'll just sit down.

Of course, there are always other seats available, which she'll notice immediately. After she looks around, but before she has a chance to say anything, I jump in. "Okay, you got me, but I was just thinking to myself—here's another lunch break and instead of munching on a doughnut and sipping some coffee as usual, why don't I do something different, maybe a bit crazy, and meet someone new, right out of the blue, for example? Have you ever had those thoughts? Of doing something crazy at times?" Sure she has. Now ask: "What kind? When was the last time you had any? Crazy thoughts, I mean? What did you do?" And voilà—you are in conversation!

By the way, whenever you suddenly find yourself saying something with a double meaning to it, for example, "When was the last time you had any?" in the above conversation, be sure to draw her attention to the double meaning by correcting yourself or specifying what you meant. She may not even have noticed the double meaning at first, but now that you've corrected yourself, she'll be sure to also think of that other meaning. But neither can she really fault you for anything, because the double meaning was purely "accidental." Getting the girl to think about sex without her actually being able to blame you for provoking her is one of the golden tools of pick-up. For more classic double entendres, watch some Bond movies, especially the parts where Bond talks with all those women he keeps meeting.

If you live in a fairly large town, there are probably ten coffee places within easy driving distance. Why not visit two a week and practice this technique? You'll be amazed how well it works (and how many great-looking women hang out alone in coffee shops)—and how painless it is when it doesn't.

STEP **15**

# Talkers vs. Listeners

As a newbie, listeners will throw you because
you'll be wondering: "Is she a listener, or is she
blowing me off?" . . . When you first start out,
always assume the woman is a listener; that will
keep you from bailing on a lot of games you could
have won.

After a few rounds in the seduction ring, you're going to realize
there are two types of women out there: talkers and listeners.

Talkers are easy. They dominate the conversation. All you
have to do is drop them a question every now and then to keep
them going and listen to their responses. Of course, *asking* and
*listening* aren't just words, they are specific techniques you need
to master so that you can take the conversation from meaningless to seduction in the shortest amount of time possible. But
we'll get to that later.

Listeners are harder . . . at first. Listeners give short answers
and hardly ever ask questions; they want to be led everywhere.
Once you are experienced with women, listeners won't be a
problem. You'll know exactly which questions to ask them to fig-

ure out who they are and what they really want. Then you'll use that information to become the man of their dreams.

But that's down the road. As a newbie, listeners will throw you because you'll be wondering: "Is she a listener, or is she blowing me off?" Listeners will make you nervous because they are not expressive or responsive. So when you first start out, always assume the woman is a listener; that will keep you from bailing on a lot of games you could have won.

What? That's a lame, cop-out piece of advice? Okay, here's the best tip for figuring out whether you've hooked a listener or a blow-off artist: her eyes. Is she looking at you, at the table, or down at her drink? If so, she's not blowing you off.

I'm not talking about eye contact. Many people (and women are people, too) have trouble with eye contact. She's probably looking down and away because she's nervous. What you want to avoid is a woman who is looking around, her eyes actively searching the surrounding area, while you are talking. That's a clear sign she is searching for something better. It's not an end to the encounter, but you'd better get her focused quickly or you're wasting your time. The more she's looking around, the faster you need to get to Step Sixteen.

# Starting the Conversation

> Have at least one other open-ended, follow-up
> question in mind, and preferably more, so that you
> don't stall out.

Whatever your approach—whether a simple hello, a cheesy pickup line (though I'd caution against that unless you enjoy an uphill battle), or a standard opener like the Opinion Approach)—the first words out of your mouth are the bridge that takes you from stranger to conversation. Remember, it's the bridge, not the destination.

The key to the approach is to end it with a question that will get her into conversation. This doesn't mean that your first words should be a question—you can always go with a funny comment or observation—but you can never let it dangle without something to prompt her to respond. Remember, seduction is about positive interaction. The sequence is:

1. Use an opener to initiate contact.
2. In case the opener itself wasn't an open-ended question, *immediately* follow it up with a question that she'll have to answer with more than a yes or no. Open-ended questions usually begin with "what," "how," or "why."

3.  Have at least one other open-ended, follow-up question in mind, and preferably more, so that you don't stall out. However, if you don't have any questions or follow-ups in mind, don't make that an excuse not to approach. Don't worry, soon enough the follow-up questions and comments will start flowing naturally and stemming from the conversation itself.

4.  And that's it. Open, question, follow-up—and you're in conversation!

It's not always that easy, of course, and tonight is one of those nights when it isn't. The best thing about the Opinion Opener is that no matter how hard she tries, it's difficult not to respond to the question "What's your opinion on . . . ?" People just love to give their opinions, especially on subjects that matter to them or in which they consider themselves to be experts.

After she's given you her opinion on whatever and the conversation still doesn't get a kick-start from it, you can steal a line from the familiar opening: "Hey, you look kind of familiar, are you from around here?" If she says she's not, you can still end this with "Well I could have sworn I've seen you before," and then ask the inevitable "So what brings you to this part of the world?" But if she says she's a local, all the better. "I'm from here too, born and bred. We must have seen each other somewhere before. Do you work out at a gym?"

You've got her in a perfect position now. You've created familiarity because you're both locals; you've suggested you have a lot in common; you've implied you work out a lot and are in good shape; and you've turned the conversation to her interests.

By the way, you don't have to suggest a gym. It could be going to the park, a favorite restaurant, even church (risky, and definitely only to be used if you actually go to church). The goal is to suggest something that reflects positively on both you and her.

# Smile

You know that old tag line: Never let them see you sweat? That's good advice, but here's some even better advice: Never let them see you fret.

What is the most important element of the approach? How do you turn a girl that has started off cold and uninterested? How do you keep a conversation going even when she's trying to shut it down?

Smile. Just keep smiling.

You might think this is simplistic advice, but you'll be amazed how easy it is to turn cranky and negative if a conversation doesn't start out on fire. You know that old tag line: Never let them see you sweat? That's good advice, but here's some even better advice: Never let them see you fret.

Never complain about the bar.

Never complain about your life.

Never let her complain about her life. If she starts, turn the conversation toward something positive.

Never say you had a bad day.

If she asks you about your day, say "Great!" or "Fantastic!" or if it really sucked way too badly for you to be able to say that, at least come up with something like "It's getting better all the time," since that at least has to be the truth—you are, after all, having a conversation with a great lady at the moment.

But why is this so important? Because everything you say to a woman, and every physical sign you give her, will create an impression. You may think you're doing well because you're talking, but if the topic is generally negative, she's getting a negative impression of you. Nobody wants to be brought down, everyone wants to be cheered up. Nobody likes a whiner but everybody likes a winner. Stay positive, stay interesting and interested, and you're well on your way.

A word of warning, though. Cheering a woman up does *not* involve solving her problems for her. This is a common beginner mistake. You start thinking, "Wow, this girl is fucked up. If I just hear her out and give her some good advice, she's going to be so thankful she's gonna want to make love to me right here and now." Nope, she's not. Sure, she's going to be thankful, but most certainly not in the way you wanted her to be. She is now thankful to you for having solved whatever problem she was having and she just found herself a nice, friendly, problem-solving friend. *Friend.* Yeah. And that does not include sex. Not now, not ever. She can have sex with anyone but problem-solving friends are hard to find. Now that she's found one, she's going to want to keep you as such. No way is she going to risk losing a precious problem-solving friend to get yet another lover, so once you start solving her problems for her, you can kiss your dreams of ever having sex with her good-bye. Sad but true.

Just get her mind off her problems by being engaging, entertaining, and interesting (and you'll be able to get her off later on for even more entertainment). The number one method of giving her a friendly problem-free interaction is to both approach with a smile and to smile every once in a while during the conversation. Even without cause if you have to.

# Signal In/Signal Away

> My body language is essential in making a
> connection with a woman. I need to show her I'm
> strong, masculine, and caring without being too
> forward. I want to create intimacy, but not push
> her too far.

Let's step back a minute, because while I'm trying to get this conversation started with this beautiful woman, I'm also doing something else: I'm using my body language to send her messages of confidence, security, sincerity, interest, and, yes, sexuality. (Meanwhile, her body is sending me some very clear messages back, but we'll get into that later.)

My body language is essential in making a connection with a woman. I need to show her I'm strong, masculine, and caring without being too forward. I want to create intimacy, but not push her too far. It might seem like a difficult line to walk, but once you've spent some real time with real women, it's not that hard to figure out how to make your body send the right messages at the right time.

One of the best devices for doing this is Signal In/Signal Away. This isn't a gimmick; it's an important technique that you'll learn to use subconsciously after a few months of practice. Don't worry, women never catch on to it, even when you're a beginner!

The technique is basically this: When you say something positive, or something you want associated with yourself, you signal toward yourself. The easiest way to do this is to put your hand on your chest. When you say something negative, signal away from yourself. The easiest way to do this is to look away and swipe your hand out to the side with your palm facing away from you.

I might say, "Sure, some guys just want to use women to stroke their own egos, but a lot of men sincerely want to get to know interesting, exciting, and enthusiastic people." I signal away on the first part (that's not me) and signal in on the second part. The signal in not only implies that I'm sincere in my attentions, but that I'm an interesting, exciting, and enthusiastic person.

Does this really work? It's not going to get her to jump right in bed, but Signal In/Signal Away definitely gives me an advantage in planting the right ideas in her mind and rooting the wrong ideas out. Don't ever underestimate the power of subconscious signals; if you try to seduce only with words, you're just going to be blowing a lot of hot air without anyone there to feel it.

# Respect and "Violate" Her Personal Space

> Some time in the first three questions (usually the
> third), I don't hear her response. Okay, I heard
> them all, but I *act* like I didn't hear one of them. So
> what do I do? I lean in really close, touch her
> lightly on the back or shoulder, and ask her to
> repeat herself.

I always start an encounter by standing instead of sitting. The
woman is sitting at the bar, and there's an open seat next to her,
but I stand between the empty seat and her seat. And no slouching, of course. Slouching is for self-doubting schmoes; I want to
come across as confident and in control. As an added bonus,
good posture makes me appear taller and better looking. And
I'm standing over her (above her), which gives me the position
of power. Subconsciously, women love men who take the position of power.

Sure, there's a danger of looking like a tight-ass with a pinecone up your behind, but a friendly smile is the perfect antidote

for this. Just make it look natural; don't stand like a stiff. If you've developed true confidence, this won't be a problem.

When I approach a woman, I always give her three feet of room (about the length of your arm)—no more, no less. As I talk with her, asking her questions about her hometown, her hobbies, and her childhood, I close that gap until I'm about eighteen inches away. Inside eighteen inches is her personal space—you have to do some work before you can get in there, but once she lets you in without pulling back, stay there. That's your zone.

Some time in the first three questions (usually the third), I don't hear her response. Okay, I heard them all, but I *act* like I didn't hear one of them. So what do I do? I lean in really close, touch her lightly on the back or shoulder, and ask her to repeat herself. Then, after she repeats herself, I lean back to my original position and ask her another question.

What have I done? I've entered her private space, but have done so in a very nonthreatening way. I've created powerful intimacy, but because I had a good reason and was brief in my flirtation, I haven't offended her.

And I've touched her—the most powerful seduction tool known to man. There is nothing more powerful than an appropriate yet sensual physical touch. If she leans into the touch, even slightly, she's liking it. It doesn't matter what other signals she is sending, or how uninterested she seems in the conversation, touching back is the only signal that matters.

If you think she responded, touch her again. The easiest, and least offensive way to do this is to sit down (Be sure to pull the chair toward her, you don't want to go backward!) and graze her leg with your foot. If she doesn't pull away, you are locked in.

With the lean in and touch, I've also called her bluff. This girl hasn't been engaging me the whole time. Now I've called her out and basically said outright, "If you want to talk, you're going to have to pay more attention to me." I've given her the choice. If she's just being shy (unintentionally distant) or cautious (intentionally distant but not committed to it), I've given her the perfect chance to engage in the conversation.

Another way to enter her personal space is lead her to do the action herself. Instead of stepping into her personal space, just pull her into yours. Unlike in the above example, where you understandably have to pull back and lean away after the brief approach, after you've pulled the woman closer to you, you can just let her stay there. Even though you pulled her in, she feels like she is the aggressor and therefore is a lot more comfortable being this close to you. After all, she entered your space, not the other way around.

Even without actually pulling her in you can lead her to come closer to you by talking to her in a loud environment in which she can't quite hear you. She has no option other than to step closer in order to hear you better. And make sure you keep talking to her even though it may be obvious she's not hearing you—eventually she *will* want to hear you better.

One last thing, which is a perfect bridge between talking about my body language and talking about hers: the Head Tilt. Books on body language tell us when a woman is interested in a conversation, she tilts her head. If you tilt your head when you listen to a woman, it helps to convey to her that you're interested in what she's saying, even if you aren't. And it works even though the woman may not consciously realize that you're tilting your head. So ask some of your follow-up questions with a slight tilt of your head. She will find you a lot more sincere and will be more eager to converse with you as a result.

# Read Her Body Language

The important thing to notice is whether she is *more* open after a few minutes or not. She doesn't have to be completely open after two minutes but any sign of movement is enough of a reason to continue with the seduction.

After two minutes, you should have enough information to be able to read the girl and tell how the conversation is going. Almost all women start in a closed, defensive position—arms crossed or close to the body, shoulders turned away. Actually, most men do this too, so always be conscious of your position and approach in an open manner. Keep your arms away from your body—never cross them on your chest. As you start the conversation, stand beside her. People feel less threatened by people next to them than right in front of them. Also make sure you aren't directly facing her in the beginning either. It should look like you're just conversing casually and not mounting a full attack. As she gets more comfortable with you, she will gradually turn toward you and you should mirror her movement. Basically, within a few minutes you should ideally have gone from talking side by side to talking while directly facing each other.

Don't forget your smile either. A smile is the most mirrored of all physical expressions. Approach without a smile and she won't smile either. Approach with a smile and she'll smile as well, even if it is just because she doesn't understand what it is you're smiling about. The smile itself will have made her feel good and since you were the cause of that, you've already scored some valuable points in her book before you even opened your mouth.

The woman described in the scenario throughout this book is seemingly not interested when I approach. That's not the important detail. The important thing to notice is whether she is *more* open after two minutes or not. She doesn't have to be completely open after two minutes but any sign of movement is enough of a reason to continue with the seduction.

This time the signs aren't good, though. Her shoulders are still turned slightly away. She hasn't turned her back on me, but what I was really hoping for was that she would turn slightly toward me so that her chest, and not her shoulder, is facing in my direction. She also still has her arms close to her body. This is a protective posture; it says "keep away." She isn't opening up to me.

She hasn't smiled. Even if she is ignoring me, a smile would tell me that the ice is only on the surface and that there's at least a little bit of warmth toward me hiding inside. But I'm getting nothing but frosty.

It's decision time.

One option is to change the direction of the approach. Clearly this conversation isn't working, but maybe there's another one that will work better. It may be time to go back to the bag of tricks and try another throw.

I don't necessarily recommend this, especially for a novice. Trying too hard feels desperate, and it can be very discouraging. The night is still young. There are many other women in the bar; why waste time?

Plus, as strange as it might seem, backing off now gives you the best opportunity to score with this woman later.

---

## I'm Flaming Out . . . Should I Offer to Buy Her a Drink?

I'll make it short and sweet: Don't buy her a drink. Ever. Don't offer to buy her a drink. Don't agree to her demands ("I'm thirsty. Will you buy me a drink?" etc.). Here's why: If you do, you supplicate. You're giving her the power, and women have nothing but scorn and disrespect for powerless men. Besides, you never want to create the expectation that you're going to buy things for her. You're not her bank. Neither do you want to create the feeling that you're trying to bribe her into talking to you. She may stay with you for the duration of downing her drink just out of pity, but once she's done with the drink, she's done with you.

Also, when a woman asks for a drink, here's what she's really thinking:

**She Says:** "Will you buy me a drink?"

**She Thinks:** *Let's see if I can hook this sucker for some free booze.*

**You Think:** *Oh boy, this woman must like me! She wouldn't ask for something free from me unless she wanted to know me better.*

**You Say:** "Sure!"

**She Thinks:** *Ha! What a wimp. Does he really think I'm gonna go to bed with him for a bottle of beer? Jeez . . . I'll take my drink and continue searching for a real man."*

**She Says:** "Thanks! You're so sweet! Oh, there's my friend over there! 'Bye."

If she stays for five or ten minutes and has a nice little chit-chat with you, that just means she's a nice person and the kind of woman you should have gotten to know *in the right way*. But you can forget it now, this encounter is already over. You got off on the wrong foot by bowing to her little power play, so she's already crossed you out in her book of prospective partners.

Buying a woman a drink will never save a flagging conversation or turn around a cold shoulder from a beautiful woman. Don't be a sucker. You're better off pitching it right back to her.

> **Her:** "I'm thirsty. Could you buy me a drink?"
> **You:** "Sorry, I don't buy drinks for women I don't know. But you could buy us both a round of drinks and then the next round is on me. How about that?"

STEP **21**

# Compliment Her Beauty?

> Everyone loves to be complimented. And do you
> know why? It gives them an ego boost. It shows
> them you want them. And why do you want them?
> Because they are better than you. Why would you
> want to tell a woman she is better than you?

Okay, I'm flailing here. I'd better pull out the big guns and go for
the direct approach. I turn toward her, look her straight in the
eyes, and say: "You have beautiful eyes. Did you know that?"

"Yes." (She's thinking: "Oh God, not another one.")

"What color are they?"

"Green." (She's thinking: "Well, that was original. Just when
I thought he was cute.")

"You know those are some of the most beautiful green eyes
I've ever seen."

"All right, now, thanks. Listen I gotta go, my friend is waiting."

Ouch. What happened?

Simply put, I made the second worst mistake I could ever
make in a seduction situation, after offering to buy her a drink. I
tried to save the encounter by complimenting her.

But don't women love to be complimented? Doesn't *everyone* love to be complimented?

Yes, everyone does love to be complimented. And do you know why? It gives them an ego boost. It shows them you want them. And why do you want them? Because they are better than you. Why would you want to tell a woman she is better than you?

You don't. In fact, this is exactly what you don't want a woman to think. Ever. You always want to be in control of a situation, a conversation, a relationship. You want the upper hand. Complimenting a woman, especially on her looks, completely strips you of power and gives it to her. Now she's got the upper hand, and you've got nothing.

If you want to comment on a woman's looks, always leave an air of insecurity about it, so that it is not exactly clear whether you actually complimented her or insulted her. For example, you could say something like "You've got nice hair. You should consider letting it grow out." You complimented her hair, then immediately implied it could be better. You lifted her up for a moment but then left her hanging, wondering which of the two you actually meant—that her hair is nice or that it could be better.

Many dedicated pick-up artists insist that gentle and joking insults about a woman's looks (especially if she is really good looking) is the best way to break down her shield and get her to be on the same level with you. That it's the ultimate way to turn the tables and gain power, especially with incredibly hot women who are used to being hit on and complimented all day long. It makes you the hunted, instead of the hunter.

The key here is not to become an asshole, though. If she takes offense, you just did that. If, however, she laughs and finds it funny, you are well on your way.

# Blow Her Off

> So many uninitiated chumps linger on forever in
> hopes of getting the girl interested, maybe,
> somehow, at some point . . . which leaves the
> bored and frustrated woman no option but to
> eject him herself. This is not good for your image
> or your self-confidence.

Remember, no individual girl is all-important! There are always more fish in the sea, and if this one isn't working out for any reason, it's your prerogative to move on to a more fruitful hunting ground.

Maybe she hasn't risen to meet your high standards. Or maybe, for whatever reason, she isn't interested. Hey, it happens all the time. If you are getting none of the signals of interest after a reasonable amount of time (five minutes) and a reasonable amount of effort (at least three attempts to start the conversation), then *simply move on.*

So many uninitiated chumps linger on forever in hopes of getting the girl interested, maybe, somehow, at some point . . . which leaves the bored and frustrated woman no option but to eject him herself. This is not good for your image or your self-confidence.

As I've said above, the girl in this example isn't opening up, so I'm cutting my losses. The important thing now is to end the conversation on a high note (leaving an opening for future interaction) and show that I'm not desperate or overeager (enhancing my image for future interaction). Hey, I offered her a hot opportunity and she failed to grasp it. I have no need to push it—I know I'm a catch and a smarter woman is going to realize that, so I just eject and move on.

Some pick-up artists also advocate a mild put-down as a parting gift with a woman who wasn't that open to your advances:

- "I'm sorry I interrupted you. I didn't realize you were so busy being miserable."

- "You know, rudeness is a sign of low self-esteem."

- "I'm sorry I tried to talk to you. Clearly I'm not even worthy of having a conversation with you because you are cooler, smarter, and better looking than the rest of us. You totally rock!"

But I recommend you use these only if she was extremely rude to you in the first place (like telling you to get lost or fuck off before you were even able to finish your first sentence). In general, though, it is best to be gracious and friendly even when you part. "It was a pleasure talking with you" or "Nice meeting you" work splendidly.

In this case, I'm still going to put a little spice in it with "I'm sorry. I didn't know you liked being alone." Why?

Well, because it's true. She is alone, and it's a bit ridiculous for someone to sit alone instead of carrying on a simple conversation. She may very well come back with "Actually, I'm waiting for some friends," which is a perfect opening to say, "Well, so am I! Why don't we wait together and I'll introduce you to my friends and you'll introduce me to yours?" Remember, even if it doesn't work out with this woman, her friends could be hot (assuming they're females, of course, but that's just the risk you'll have to take at times).

Of course, if you're really into the challenge or into this specific woman for some reason (and we're talking about a seduction here, not some kind of soul mate or "special person desperation" kind of thing) then rudeness is your last option.

That's right, if you still want this girl and you've been a nice guy up to this point, start mocking her instead, jerk. Become a jerk if you will, but a funny one, not the insulting kind. So don't overdue it, but definitely cop some attitude. Some girls only respond to guys with attitude and she might just have a change of heart and start making passes at you. Talk to her a while, then suddenly ignore her and push her away. It will make her crazy, and if she keeps at it (and you keep your cool) you'll eventually be able to do whatever you want with her.

Remember, though, that this is only a last resort and an advanced technique at that. If it doesn't work, well, she was on her way out anyway. But it may be that she turns out to be the kind of girl that likes, wants, and needs a little kick in the buttocks to develop respect for a man—and then the rude approach will have hit the jackpot.

# Find Option #2

Eventually, if you look at enough eligible girls,
one of them will lock eyes with you. When that
happens, don't look away. Hold eye contact,
even after she looks away. You want to see her
second look, too.

So far, I've played this encounter low key. I used the Three Second Rule and approached a woman right away. I gave her every opportunity to respond, but she didn't bite, so I ejected quickly while leaving the door open for future encounters.

Now what? There are two ways about it. The first is to keep going with the Three Second Rule, pick your target or group, approach, and open with your favorite opener (I recommend the Opinion Opener, since that gets the whole group engaged). The upside is that you are already in the zone, talking, moving, and interacting, and like an athlete, once the game is on, you don't want to sit on a bench or go back to the locker room to cool down until the game is over or at least until you've scored enough. If you're worried that you'll come off as a player moving from woman to woman, don't worry about it. You're just meeting people and having fun, and what could be wrong with that?

If, however, you don't feel like your skills and energy are sufficient to keep the ball continuously rolling, you can take a breather and see who's checking you out instead. Assuming I'm taking this approach, I look around with one goal in mind: I want to see who's looking at me and how they react. Eventually, if you look at enough eligible girls, one of them will lock eyes with you. When that happens, don't look away. Hold eye contact, even after she looks away. You want to see her second look, too. There is no way a woman who has locked eyes can resist glancing at you again—and her level of interest is absolutely obvious from the second glance.

Here's a simple chart for reading glances, courtesy of Don Steele (it also appears in my first book). It is more applicable to situations where you are actually interacting with a woman, but it works from across the room as well. The sequence of the list approximates the real life sequence.

| I'm Interested | Don't Bother Me |
| --- | --- |
| Sidelong glance | Never sneaks a peek |
| Looks at you again | Fleeting eye contact |
| Holds your gaze briefly | Looks away quickly |
| Downcast eyes, then away | Looks away, eyes level |
| Posture changes to alert | Posture unchanged |
| Preens, adjusts hair, attire | Does no preening |
| Turns body toward you | Turns body away |
| Tilts head | Head remains vertical |
| Narrows eyes slightly | Eyes remain normal |
| Smiles | Neutral, polite face |
| Matches your posture | Posture unchanged |
| Eyes sparkle | Normal or dull eyes |

| | |
|---|---|
| Licks her lips | Keeps mouth closed |
| Thrusts breasts | Hunches over to de-emphasize breasts |

Don't force her to maintain eye contact before making your move. Holding eye contact is almost a *guarantee* of success, but it's rarely that straightforward. If a woman holds your gaze for more than three seconds . . . *it's on!* The rest is just a formality. Move in and start a conversation—even "I noticed you looking at me" will do—and don't forget those open-ended questions. Don't worry, it was in the bag the moment you locked eyes.

If you don't seem to be getting any successful eye contact in a reasonable amount of time, cut your losses and approach the group you're interested in anyway. If you make your downtime too long, though, then like an engine, once cooled down, it will take some time to get it up to speed again. In the hectic enviroment of meeting new people, you don't want to lose momentum. If you want to rest, you can do that at home—while cuddling with your new-found female companion.

Let's assume I eventually catch a girl making eye contact. I keep our gazes locked. She glances at me again, then looks down and away. Good. Down and away means she's noticed me and she *cares* what I think of her. As soon as she does that, no hesitation. I'm up and after her.

But there's one catch: she's with a group of four other women. Big problem, right? Not at all.

---

### What If She's Still Nervous After Strong Initial Eye Contact?

Meaningless. Absolutely meaningless. Don't be put off by nervousness, her ignoring you, or even put-downs (especially if she's with a group of other girls). You already know she's interested because you noticed her looking at you. But being approached and being talked to is a big step up from just holding eye contact. She may be worried how you perceive her from closer up, or what people (her friends and strangers) will think if she's instantly flirtatious with a strange guy. There's a bit of nervousness and self-consciousness in almost everyone when meeting and talking to someone new, and most girls have been raised with the belief that if they don't play a little hard to get, then they're slutty. Just let it slide, let it subside, don't pay any attention to it, and it should go away within the first few minutes of talking to her.

# Approach the Group

Approaching a group of females may seem like the ultimate in macho—after all, you're throwing yourself to the hungry pack and, when together, animals tend to get vicious with an intruder, right? Actually, no. Approaching a group of women is not any harder than approaching one woman. In fact, it's probably even easier!

Many guys approach a group with a basic "Hi ladies, how are you tonight?" I bet they've never been asked that before. Well, of course that's better than not approaching a group at all or approaching a group and falling flat on your face—literally slipping on a banana peel or something on your way over there. But seriously, that's as boring a question as it gets and it'll yield you as boring an answer in return ("Yeah, fine, thanks" while looking away), so why would you want to make things harder on yourself than they need to be? Sure, if Brad Pitt came over and asked them that very same question, they'd be all excited, but that's because it was Brad Pitt asking the question. Unless you're Brad Pitt, that question is hardly going to create much interest in the ladies.

Remember, a player has to be the *exception* to the rules. If every other guy approaches them with "So how are you tonight?" that's the very thing you have to avoid.

So now that the crowd favorite has been voted down, what do you do? Strange as it seems, you can start with a simple "Hi," but not for the purposes of waiting for the other party to respond before proceeding. Just say "Hi" and see who answers. Those who do probably like you already. Those who don't, you'll need to become friends with later on if the girl you're interested in is not among them, or use special tactics if she is.

For now, a "Hi" will suffice, but don't depend on getting an answer. They may all just give you a puzzled look without saying anything and you must not give an impression that your "Hi" was actually a question asking for their permission to continue speaking to them. So without even looking like you were expecting any responses (just note who responded and who didn't), proceed with an Opinion or Familiar Opener.

Let's say in this case I'm still getting the cold group shoulder (I'm having a harsh night, aren't I). They answer, but not particularly enthusiastically. That's not unusual. They may be in "girls' night out" mode where they just want to be left alone. Also, none of the girls want to speak for the group and let you in—except the girl who's been making eye contact, and she's the last to talk because she doesn't want her friends to know she brought you over.

But here's what makes approaching a group relatively easy: You don't have to impress everybody. You only need to get okayed by one member to be in, then you can proceed to being okayed by the rest of the group.

So I should start chatting to the girl who made eye contact, right? After all, she obviously wants to talk with me.

Nope.

I never start chatting with the object of my affection in a group situation. In fact, I always plan to talk to her last. First, I want to make a good impression on her friends. And to do that,

I select the female member of the group who looks the most bored and start chatting with her.

> "You look like you're having fun. Did they drag you out here against your will?"
> "Yeah, because I was worried about meeting guys like you."
> "You mean fun-loving guys who want to talk to you?"

This is just friendly banter. The goal is to be fun, spontaneous, and non-threatening. Do not try to pick her up. She may not be interested in you (she may be a sourpuss, which was why she wasn't having any fun in the first place), but your presence will bring out the competitive juices in all the other women there. And pretty soon, you'll get to know them all.

Now in case you *did* make eye contact with the girl you were interested in from across the room, keep making as much eye contact as possible with that girl. We haven't said a word, but we're already into a heavy flirtation. If, however, you did a cold approach, just ignore the girl you're actually interested in for now. Most likely she's the prettiest in the group and is used to being sucked up to from the get-go, but now all of a sudden this guy approaches the group who's not paying any attention to her at all. That'll be something new for her to ponder and it'll get her intrigued and wondering about you soon enough.

---

### The Self-Selecting Group Dynamic: God's Gift to Men

If I can't find a girl making eye contact with me, and it's a seduction situation, I always approach a group. Why? Because groups are self-selecting.

What do I mean by that? I mean that with a group you have multiple chances to meet a woman who is open to be seduced, and the group dynamic will bring her out quicker than a mouse to cheese.

In a group, if one of the other women is interested in you, even slightly, she will let it be known by giving you eye contact or trying to join the conversation. If that doesn't happen, the other members of the group will often point you, subconsciously, to the woman most in need of a guy like you in their opinion, either by dropping hints, nudging the girl, or trying to bring her forward to speak. This is what I mean by self-selecting on the part of the group, and it's the real secret to why group dynamics are such a good way to meet women.

And of course, there's no reason why you shouldn't give this process a little shove as well. In other words, why wait for the available girl to show herself when you can easily draw her out?

As soon as I've been introduced around, and everyone's starting to feel comfortable, I jump right into a leading question, such as, "I'm curious. Which one of you has the most inquisitive and adventurous mind?" Almost always, the group will volunteer a girl. And you know who she'll be? The one they think you should be with! She may not be the most attractive girl in the group (and remember you can always eject later if you're really not interested in her), but she's definitely going to be the one who is available.

# Disarm the Friend

> It's especially important to befriend the disapproving girl (who is usually the ugly one as well, no big surprise here) because she probably holds the moral strings on this crowd and isn't afraid to pull them at all the wrong times.

After a few minutes (or often even within thirty seconds), one girl usually emerges in every group. She's the talker, and she's your biggest obstacle. Technically, an obstacle is every person in the group who isn't your target. But in reality there are only two obstacles to worry about: the moral compass and the talker.

An ignored talker is a dangerous obstacle. She is pissed by the dis, and will only get more pissed the longer the conversation continues. She considers herself the most outgoing and interesting member of the group, so if you ignore her you must just be here for sex—and since you clearly don't want to have sex with her, she's going to try to thwart you at every turn.

Remember, the target's friends have far more influence over her than you can hope to achieve in ten minutes of brilliant banter, which means if the talker starts to interfere with your pickup by dragging the target away, talking with her and ignoring you, or making rude comments and breaking the mood . . . you're dead meat. If you're really good, the target may slip you her phone number on the fly as she's being dragged out of your life. More likely, the obstacle's poisonous tongue will have ruined your chances forever.

That's why successful men always befriend the obstacles *before* the target. Being friends with her friends makes you look good, so spread yourself around, and have a good time doing it. Shake hands, be humorous, give a few "I understand where you're coming from" nods. Play along with their jokes at your expense. It's especially important to befriend the disapproving girl (who is usually the ugly one as well, no big surprise here) because she probably holds the moral strings on this crowd and isn't afraid to pull them at all the wrong times for you. Befriend her, play games with her, make her like you, and then, only then, turn your attention for the first time to the target.

Not only have you disarmed the obstacles, you've disarmed your target as well. Since your target is no doubt the most attractive female in the group (or at least very good looking), she is used to being the center of attention with men. But here you are, ignoring her, in front of everyone! She thought she had a good thing going, but now she's confused and, of course, really wanting you to pay attention to her.

And that is the perfect time to make your move.

---

### The PUA Quiz: Get This Right, and You're Halfway Home

**Questions:** A pretty girl and an ugly girl are standing together in a bar. Who do you talk to first?

**Answer:** Always talk to the ugly girl first.

**Reason:** The hot girl will be surprised, jealous, and intrigued. Now she's going to try that much harder to win you over. And the ugly girl is positively surprised as well. She's used to being ignored; therefore, you must be a really nice guy. In fact, she may decide you're a better match for her hot girlfriend—and you've just made an unexpected but insanely powerful ally! But even if she won't become an active ally, she most certainly won't become your active obstacle, which she would have become if you had ignored her in the first place.

STEP **26**

# Get Separation

Now that I've disarmed the friends, I take the
first opportunity to separate her from the rest
of the group.

Sooner or later I will need to get some separation. I need to separate my target (the girl I'm actually interested in) from all the
other guys in the room and also from her girlfriends. I can do
this in a number of ways. Once I've befriended the general
group, entertained her less interesting friends for a while, and
have been okayed by them, the conversation may break into
smaller parts and by now I've been able to maneuver to get beside her. If I haven't (sometimes it is physically impossible) well,
what the heck, I can still address her from wherever I am. Ideally, though, I should be between her and the rest of the
room/her friends/other guys. If that's the case and we're talking, great. If she seems to have sufficiently warmed up to me, I
can say: "Hey, I want you to meet a friend of mine, I think you
two would really get along." If she seems apprehensive at first, I
talk at length about the amazing qualities and achievements of
my friend, how everyone loves and respects him (or her) and
why, until she can no longer object to meeting such a wonderful

person. To the rest of the group I can say, "I'll just borrow her for a sec, I'll introduce her to a friend of mine, we'll be back in an instant." If her friends wonder whether they can come along, I say, "Sure, when we (I and my chosen girl from the group) find him, we'll bring him right back here so you can all meet him." Notice how I didn't really answer the question I was asked ("Can we come along?"), but rather a question I wanted to anwer ("Can we meet him?"), which sort of answered the question, but never really addressed the uncomfortable issue of having her friends drag along.

Keep in mind that women usually don't like to leave their group of friends with a guy they just met even if they like the guy. They're too concerned about how that'll look to their friends. However, when you state your reasons for leaving with her and promise to be back in an instant, you'll make it a lot easier for her to come along with you.

So who on earth is this friend I'm talking about? Well if I really did come with a friend, that'd be him. However since in this scenario I came alone, I can either use whomever I met at the bar before approaching this group (even the unresponsive woman I had to eject will do in a pinch), but better yet, I can just pretend to be looking for that friend and naturally we'll have to keep looking and keep looking. All the while I'm walking around with this beauty, we can chat, stop here and there, etc. And even if we never find the friend (and we won't, since I didn't bring anyone with me), all the other women at the bar don't know that. All they see is me walking around with this gorgeous girl by my side and a sight like that can do wonders for their interest toward me.

At some point it will become obvious that the friend isn't there. I will of course act accordingly: "You know, I'm really worried about my friend. I guess I need to go outside, make a phone call, hopefully he'll pick up the phone and I'll find out what's up. But listen . . . I've really had a great time and in case I have to run out and save my friend's ass from some trouble he hopefully has not gotten himself into, I want you to know . . . I just have to tell you that . . ." Now I give her a good, sincere compliment that has nothing to do with her beauty or anything else painfully obvious about her, such as telling her that her conversation skills really keep me listening, and follow up with "I hope you're the kind of woman who can tell the difference between a casual comment (I gesture away like that's clearly not my game) and a sincere observation (I point to myself). And I'd love to continue this conversation at some later point. How can we do that?"

Notice how I let *her* come up with offering me her phone number or some other means of contacting her. If however she's at a loss for words, I'm not phased by it and tell her: "Okay, I really gotta go make that phone call and then I probably have to run someplace else, but why don't you give me your phone number and I'll call you tomorrow so we can pick it up where we left off."

# Walk Away

Seduction offers many opportunities to walk away
a winner, and I always give the same advice: As
soon as you know you're in, move immediately to
the close.

Never leave a conversation because the girl is losing interest.
Does this mean you should continue babbling even though she
is quite obviously bored? No, this means you should have left
*before* she got bored! Failing to exit at the right moment is one of
the cardinal sins of seduction. You should always leave at the
high point of the conversation, when she's still fascinated by
you. This is especially true if you've already made the necessary
arrangements like extracting her phone number or agreeing to
meet up later.

In this encounter, I look directly into her eyes for as long as
she will hold my gaze . . . and then tell her I have to leave. This
will confuse the hell out of her and make her intrigued, but more
important, I'm leaving her wanting more.

At this point, I skip directly to Step Fifty-five, the Number
Close, and my work for tonight (at least at this bar) is done. End
of story. End of book.

What? You still want more?

Okay, okay. A better option, if you want to continue instead of closing, is to skip the whole "I gotta call my friend and probably leave, so give me your number" route and opt for "Oh well, I guess he left for a moment. He sometimes does that, but I'm sure he'll be back, so why don't we go to the balcony/that corner table and chat until he shows up." Then take her gently by the elbow and guide her to a corner table to talk. Since this is a book, not an actual seduction, let's say I go that route tonight. After all, I've still got forty tips to share.

STEP **28**

# Dance?

Kino girls hate talking, so don't waste your time.
Chances are, while you're laying down your lines,
she'll be wondering why you aren't touching her.
Not reading a woman right and making her
frustrated is classic chump.

Let me take this opportunity, while I'm leading my partner of
the moment toward a corner table or a balcony, to talk about an
important aspect of the pickup scene: dancing.

Throughout history, dancing has been a pre-copulation ritual
and a primary test for choosing a mate. If you're good, dancing
is a great way to attract women. Just slip in with the most beautiful women and you'll get their attention plus the attention of
everyone else on and off the floor.

But let's face it: Most of us aren't great dancers. That's one of
the main reasons a dance club is not a great place to meet
women (the others are that they're expensive and often too loud
for intimate conversation). One option is to put a lot of time
and effort into becoming a good dancer. I'm not saying this is a
bad idea and as a bonus it will probably help you with your hor-

izontal moves between the sheets, but it's not really as necessary as you might think.

I don't really care much for dancing but that doesn't mean I don't recognize it as a useful tool and use it whenever the occasion arises. When on the floor, I always keep in mind that dancing with a woman is not my ultimate goal. It is a tool to move me closer to my real goal—getting close enough to kiss, feeling her up and tonguing her down, making her cum right there in the club, making her cum later back at my place, or even better, all of the above. The real magic of the dance is not in sweeping her off her feet, but in using those old handy tools—a smile, eye contact, and some well-timed kino.

In other words, do your dance, have fun, then get your woman off the dance floor and into a quiet, private place where you can lay it on her and make the sparks fly. As for the dancing itself, unless you are truly a Michael "Lord of the Dance" Flatley and John "Saturday Night Fever" Travolta all rolled in one, either keep it simple and just move to the rhythm—no fancy moves necessary, girls really don't pay that much attention to how a guy is dancing (unlike us guys ogling at the wiggling of the babes on the dance floor). Or if you have the personality for it, do some really exaggerated silly moves to show you have balls and a good sense of humor. Although guys will think you're a freak, girls will love you for displaying the aforementioned qualities.

The exception to these rules are the so-called "kino girls." They love being touched, and they love touching you in return. Should you encounter a girl like that (and believe me, you'll know it immediately), don't leave the dance floor. Just keep rubbing, touching, kissing, and grinding. Once the touching gets intimate, it's straight off the dance floor and into your car.

This kind of girl hates talking, so don't waste your time. Chances are, while you're laying down your lines, she'll be wondering why you aren't touching her. Not reading a woman right and making her frustrated is classic chump.

---

### Never Ask for a Dance

Is it a good idea to walk up to a girl and say, "Would you like to dance with me?" I mean, that's how your dad met your mom, so it must be a cool move. Well, it's cool only if you don't mind being shot down on face value and before the woman even gets to know you, or you're sure that the girl you're asking for a dance is also the girl you want to marry (because after all, that's what happened to your mom and dad).

When you *ask* her to dance and she says yes, great. But if she says no, you're screwed. This is a classic newbie mistake, cutting off your options and putting yourself at the mercy of someone else, this time the woman. You can try and salvage the situation by engaging her in conversation, but your interaction already started with her rejecting you, so now your job is significantly harder.

The worst part is that the rejection isn't necessarily personal. Why? Because by being a supplicating chump you let a number of factors beyond your control come into play. What if she's tired? Waiting for a friend in a designated spot? Has a boyfriend around the corner? If you supplicate, you're just encouraging her to make excuses. If you're direct and forceful, cutting off her ability to say no, then these concerns go out the window . . . as will any boyfriend stupid enough to leave a beautiful woman standing by the dance floor all alone.

You can try to save the situation by having the next woman take you up on your offer. However, the other women probably saw your crash and burn and since social proof works both ways—both positive and negative—they're now much less likely to want to do anything with you. But whatever you do, don't compound your error by standing there and arguing about why she won't dance with you. There's always a better-looking and smarter girl standing right around the corner—and you're what she's been waiting for her whole life, so stop wasting your time and hers with women who can't get with the program.

# Conversation, Part 2

**This is important, so let's review all the basics of getting a conversation started.**

We've finally reached the table, and it's time to really start talking. This is important, so let's review all the basics of getting a conversation started from my last, unsuccessful encounter. By the way, there's a very good chance that if the original woman is still alone, she'll suddenly be interested in talking to you. So talk away—but don't make the mistake of trying to pick her up just yet. Keep it light and friendly but noncommittal . . . for now.

First, I lead her with a gentle touch of the arm. Great kino!

If it's a booth or a bench, I sit on the same side of the table as she. This is more intimate, and I always know what she's looking at because I can see the same thing—not true if I'm sitting opposite her. If there's no room right next to her, I'll find the next closest place to sit. Unless it's a really small table, where your faces would end up quite close to each other, the worst place to sit is usually across the table. You get this flat horizontal wall in between the two of you and you can't put your heads together for some secret sharing or accidentally bump your thighs and leave them pressed against each other even if you wanted to.

As I talk, I maintain eye contact—remember the one-eye trick. I don't need an opener because we're past that. Instead, I ask and end with an open-ended question.

After a minute of conversation, I "unfortunately" can't hear something she says and have to lean in while touching her arm, thus entering her personal space in a nonthreatening way and making physical contact. I'll be sure to lean back, though, and after a while will talk in a way that'll make it hard for her to hear properly. The trick here is to keep talking so that she'll have to lean closer herself because if I stop, she may ask me to repeat what I said in a louder voice and then there'll be no reason for her to lean in. But if I do get her to lean in—perfect.

# Tackle the First Blocker

**She says, "You're a player, aren't you?" Uh-oh, that
sounds like trouble, right? Don't worry, it's not.**

I ask a few open-ended questions along the lines of "Are you from
around here?" "Haven't I seen you in the park?" etc.

I "can't hear" the second answer, so I lean in. She says, "You're
a player, aren't you?"

Uh-oh, that sounds like trouble, right?

Don't worry, it's not. There are many positive reasons for her
to ask this kind of question, including:

- She wants to be seduced.

- She's forward and doesn't want to waste time.

- She finds experienced guys a turn-on.

The problem is, there are also several negative reasons for
her to ask this kind of question:

- She isn't interested in a casual hookup.

- She's testing your sincerity.

- Knowing you meet a lot of women makes her feel like she's not special.

So what do you do? Your best bet, as always, is to remain a mystery. Divert her attention, make her feel special, and let her imagine you're the kind of man she wants to be with.

So instead of an outright denial, I say, "I think you're a fascinating woman, and I'd like to get to know you better. I'm drawn to a woman who has moved around as much as you have (this is a fact I elicited in the Familiar Opening). You've experienced things. I like that. But I know you must have something constant in your life that keeps you grounded. Like a pet, maybe?"

Does it work? Her actions, not just her words, will tell me.

---

### Are You Trying to Seduce Me?

This commonly asked question is one of the trickiest for guys just starting out with meeting women. It can be a dismissal; it can be a serious question where the answer she wants can either be "yes" or "no"; or it can be an invitation to sex. The key is to read her body language when she asks the question. Is she leaning in and eager for an answer? She's going to find "yes" a turn-on. Has she backed away and closed off her body, either by turning her shoulder to you or bringing her arms in close? If so, she's looking for a "no." In either case, give her the answer she wants.

Usually it's not that obvious, though, and it's best to avoid the question and remain mysterious.

# Read Her Body Language (Again)

> Within the first thirty seconds her body language
> tells me whether I'm leaving here with either a
> phone number or with this woman on my arm.

I can tell right away this conversation is going much better than the first one. In fact, within the first thirty seconds her body language tells me whether I'm leaving here with either a phone number or this woman on my arm. Here's what I see:

- She keeps looking at my face. Gorgeous women almost never do this unless they like you, so if the woman is gorgeous, this is a sure sign of interest. But this girl is pretty—an 8—so this is a good sign but not a sure thing.

- She's got a big smile with teeth showing. This shows not only that she's enjoying my company, but that she's relaxed and comfortable.

- She touches her tongue to her lips. Not in the big, sloppy, movie way, but a little brush while talking. This is a subconscious display of interest—and sexy, too. It's similar to pushing a few times at her hair. It's an unconscious attempt to make sure she's looking her best. And here's a fun thing to try: Wet and bite your lips from time to time to see if you can get a reaction from her. Wetting and biting lips are very obvious sexual signs to the subconscious mind and can elicit similar responses in the recipient of those signs.

- She mirrors my body language and body position. Since I'm open, she's open.

- She's leaning slightly forward into me, not away.

- Her hands are down and she is rubbing one of her wrists. She's open, relaxed, and exhibiting the right kind of fidgeting. Rubbing a wrist is very sexual.

- She's answering my questions.

- She's laughing.

For those of you who need a refresher on body language—or even a first course—here's a list of common positive signs. These apply both to intimate encounters and across-the-bar flirtations.

### Her Mouth

- Big relaxed smile with upper and lower teeth showing.

- Biting the lower lip or showing her tongue (especially if it's pierced!).

- She wets her lips. Some women use a single lip lick; others run the tongue around the entire area.

- She puts her fingernail between her teeth.

- She pouts her lips while thrusting her breasts forward.

### Her Eyes

- She keeps sneaking a peek at you.

- She holds your eye contact, even for a moment. When she looks away, she should look down instead of across the room.

- She raises and lowers her eyebrows, then smiles, usually with eye contact.

- She winks at you.

- She blinks more than usual, almost fluttering her eyelashes.

### Her Hair

- She pushes her hand through her hair. This can be one motion or more of a general stroking, it doesn't matter.

- She twirls her hair around her finger while looking at you.

- She throws her hair back off her shoulder.

### Her Clothing

- Her nipples are getting perky. A great sign, but for God's sake don't get fixated on them! If you happen to notice, great.

- The hem goes up to expose some leg.

- She fixes, pats, or smoothes her outfit.

### While Seated

- She moves in time with the music, with her eyes on you.

- She straightens her posture, and her muscles appear to tense.

- Her legs are open.

- Her legs are crossed in a manner that reveals her inner thigh.

- Her legs are rubbing against each other.

- Her crossed leg is pointed toward you. Often, she will be rocking it gently toward you as well.

### Her Hands

- She exposes the palm of her hand.

- She rests her elbow in the palm of her hand, while holding out or gesturing with the other hand palm up.

- She lowers her drink. This is an invitation to come in closer.

- Her hands are steady and not fidgeting with keys, straws, glasses, etc.

- She rubs her wrists.

- One hand is touching one of her breasts.

- She touches her cheek briefly. If she leaves her hand there, it's a bad sign.

- She plays with her jewelry, especially with a stroking or light pulling motion. If she's pinching or yanking, bad sign.

- She touches you while talking.

- She looks away and pretends to check her watch as you pass her.

### Her Voice

- She raises or lowers the volume of her voice to match yours.

- She speeds up or slows down her speech to match your pace.

- She laughs in unison with you.

- In a crowd, she speaks only to you and focuses her undivided attention on you.

### Other

- She mirrors your body language and body position.

- Her skin reddens, especially her ears or cheeks.

- She leans over and whispers in her friend's ear, just like in junior high.

- She is standing with her head cocked at a slight angle, one foot behind the other, hips thrust slightly forward.

- You keep bumping into her "accidentally" or you catch her glancing at you. Or more subtly, she may just happen to keep positioning herself near you over the course of ten or twenty minutes.

But be warned: These signals work with most beautiful women, but the really gorgeous, knockout model types very seldom bother to display any such signs of interest at all. Why? Because they've never had to, so they've never learned them, either consciously or subconsciously. With these women, you have to be alert for more subtle signs of interest.

# Calibrate the Girl

> As soon as I get a chance, I deliberately, but
> naturally during the flow of conversation, say
> things I know will get positive and negative
> reactions, then look for how those reactions
> manifest themselves.

Paying attention to her reactions can give you a general idea of how things are going, but how do you know what she's really thinking? Well, essentially, you ask. I call this "calibrating the girl," or finding out exactly how her face and body react to display both happiness and sadness.

As soon as I get a chance, I deliberately, but naturally during the flow of conversation, say things I know will get positive and negative reactions, then look for how those reactions manifest themselves.

When I ask what keeps her grounded, this girl mentions a cat. A cat is perfect for calibration!

I say, "I had a cat when I was a kid. I loved her very much, but she got outside once and the neighbor's dog apparently got a bite out of her or something, since she had bite marks on her when she got back. She died a few weeks later. I never could quite get over it." Substitute this for some sad story of your own, because trust me, you do not want to make up stories that aren't true. First, you'll never be able to keep track of your lies (what you've told and to whom) and second, sooner or later all lies are inevitably revealed as such and that's always a major source of embarrassment.

Now watch the way her facial expression immediately changes and her posture shifts. That's how she looks when she's sad or uncomfortable. Save that knowledge for later!

"I'm so sorry."

I pause for a second, as if thinking about the cat. Then I say something positive: "It's great when your cat comes in and wakes you up in the morning, isn't it?"

Watch her closely for that subconscious reaction. Now I know her personal expression of a positive, happy emotion—exactly what I want to see on her face all night.

These examples may sound silly—you may think you already know what happy and sad look like—but you'll find that the entire face and the entire body display emotion, and this complex body language is unique to each girl. A poor chump thinks only a smile or a frown conveys emotion, but you're looking for *all* of the signs that the girl gives off. Once you're in seduction mode, watch for those signs: They're mileposts on your ride to the promised land.

STEP **33**

# Pace Her Ongoing Reality

> You have absolutely nothing to expect from a girl
> to whom you do not demonstrate value and
> personality. You have to show her something of
> interest, something that makes her like the way
> she feels around you. This is the entire basis of
> seduction.

By now, after two minutes, I'm over the hump and into a genuine conversation. Now my goal—and listen up, because this is
important—is to demonstrate value and personality.

You have absolutely nothing to expect from a girl to whom
you do not demonstrate value and personality. You have to
show her something of interest, something that makes her like
the way she feels around you. This is the entire basis of seduction.

But how do you do this? Easy. You build rapport and make a
connection by showing you have a lot in common. Yes, I've
heard how opposites attract and that's all fine, but in the end
commonalities unite people faster and bind them closer together
than differences, so that's what I suggest you base your approach on. Or if you find yourself thinking: "But I don't even

know this girl! How can I make sure I don't say something she disagrees with?" then don't worry, we'll get to that in a moment.

You need to start by first pacing her ongoing reality. I always use this technique when making fluff talk—the conversational bridge between the opening and eliciting values (more on that to come)—and I recommend it to you, especially if you're a beginner.

Pacing her ongoing reality means talking about what is actually going on right at the moment. In other words, talk about the thing you have in common—this bar and the two minutes you've already spent talking. She can't disagree with that, can she? And that's when you take it to the next level.

First, I describe the very recent past. I don't want to remind her about her friends, who are still across the bar, so I mention the eye contact we made. This is demonstrably true—we did make eye contact—so there's no way she can disagree. Plus, I've turned the conversation to us and shown that I'm attentive.

Next I describe the ongoing reality—the fact that I am talking to her right now. Again, this is something she can't possibly disagree with because it's true. I am sitting right here talking to her.

Now I move on to mention how much we have in common (a love of cats, for example) and how much fun this conversation is. Not only am I creating an atmosphere of honesty, simplicity, and enthusiasm for the moment, but I'm talking about our shared experience and framing the experience in a positive way.

What if she's not having a good time? If the discrepancy is minor, this kind of talk can overcome her hesitation and convince her that, yes, she is having fun and you do have a lot in common.

If her body language is telling you she is really not agreeing at all, then you'd better change the subject. You're overselling it, and you're about to pull the hook right out of the fish's mouth.

Finally, I describe the immediate future—the fact that she

will continue to feel good about meeting someone new and interesting. This is the kicker. I've built rapport by telling her stuff that is clearly true, and now I'm subtly switching to suggesting something I want to be true. She's agreed with me on several things already, so she is likely to agree with a few more statements, even if, objectively speaking, they may or not actually be true.

What have I done here? I've shown her my honesty and sincerity, and how many things we have in common. I've got her thinking about my positive qualities, and once I've done that, I'm well on my way to success.

But I'm being subtle. I'm not overloading her with things she probably won't agree with, and I don't rush to the third step if I haven't nailed down the first two. My goal is to keep a balance between truth and suggestion, always pushing her "reality" a bit past the actual in a positive direction. If I push too hard she'll stop agreeing . . . and then bye-bye rapport, bye-bye love.

---

### Conversation No-Nos

- Your personal problems (family, work, money)
- Her personal problems. Never offer her life advice.
- Previous girlfriends—especially anything about how they mistreated you, dumped you, cheated on you, took you to the cleaners on child support, etc.
- Her previous boyfriends
- Health problems and ailments—yours and hers. Also death is a complete taboo topic.
- Anything negative. Complaining about the vodka, the music, or the crowd doesn't make you seem intelligent and sophisticated, it makes you seem like a grump.

- Politics, religion, and conspiracy theories. Always agree with her if she brings them up, then change the subject.

- Bragging, unless it's casually dropped in as part of a strategy outlined in this book. Bragging makes you seem insecure and insincere. If she "forces" you to brag about yourself by asking you about something in particular, answer as if you're a bit ashamed to talk about this great aspect of your life. Let her discover your successes on her own and they will become much larger for her. But try to force them down her throat and they will immediately be diminished in her eyes. Besides it is always preferable to talk about her, not yourself.

- If you aren't funny, don't try to be. Just be friendly and smile.

And watch the alcohol! Drunkenness really makes a bad impression. Try not to drink; if you must, have at most a couple of drinks a night.

STEP **34**

# Control the Conversation

You must always make sure the conversation is
going somewhere. Make sure everything you
say has a reason, that it's leading to . . . well, you
know where you want this conversation to go:
relationships, intimacy, sex, and then the chance to
turn those words into action.

Lots of guys don't have a clue what they're trying to do when
they talk to a woman. Their thinking is this: "As long as I'm talking to her, that's a good thing! The longer I talk, the better my
chances!" So they pepper the poor woman with questions—
"Where you goin'?" "What you doin'?" "What'd you do yesterday?"—that are nothing more than aimless and desperate small
talk.

That is a mistake. This kind of conversation is only margin-
ally better than not having a conversation at all. Spending too
much time talking with the woman will actually hurt your
chances of success. You're just giving yourself an opportunity to
say something wrong; you're creating the impression that you
have noplace else to go; and eventually, no matter how long you

can keep afloat a conversation that only goes around in circles and has no real meaning to her, she's going to grow tired of you.

You must always make sure the conversation is going somewhere. Make sure everything you say has a reason, that it's leading to . . . well, you know where you want this conversation to go: relationships, intimacy, sex, and then the chance to turn those words into action.

Facts are boring. They aren't particularly personal, and they don't have much meaning. What I am after is feelings and sensations. I want to get her thinking about her body and her emotions. What I'm really looking for is something special to her, something that makes her feel wonderful. When I find that thing, I latch on to it—whether it's the rush of wind while she's ice skating or the thought of her cat licking her face. I create a personal bond based on her intimate beliefs or experiences.

So I ask a simple question: "Do you have a favorite hobby?"

She says, "Not really."

"Come on. There's nothing you like to do?"

"Well, I like rollerblading, but I'm not very good at it. And I really love to go skiing."

Great. Here's where I make it personal and turn the dialogue from facts to sensations. "I've been skiing a few times. Don't you just love that feeling of gliding down the mountain, hardly putting any effort into your movement, just going where momentum takes you? There's so much freedom. And then you speed up, and with almost every inch of your body you can feel the sensation of flying. You can feel your heart rate speeding up and the tingle all over your body. I just absolutely love that feeling, don't you?"

(By the way, I've never been skiing in my life. I'm just sticking some basic positive feelings and emotions into her personal setting.)

In essence, I've just asked the age-old, boring question, "What do you like to do?" A chump, though, wouldn't even bother listening to her reply, and would probably just continue with "Uh-huh, great" because he was already thinking how to make his own favorite pastimes (drinking beer and watching sports) sound more interesting.

Unlike that chump, I was listening to what mattered to her and was able to create instant rapport based on her answer. And my answer was both personal and sensual. I worked in positive emotions, a pounding heart, a tingling all over the body . . . and of course the pleasure you get from having the freedom to do what you want.

I think you know what other activity has those associations.

# Mirror Her

Verbal mirroring is wonderful, but there is an even
more powerful mirroring tool available in every
seduction scenario: physical mirroring.

Echoing back the woman's attitudes and interests is called "mirroring": I am making myself a mirror in which she can see herself
reflected back.

Verbal mirroring is wonderful, but some smarter and more
experienced women (exactly the kind you want to meet!) may
pick up on it because they focus on your words. There is an even
more powerful, nearly undetectable mirroring tool available in
every seduction scenario: physical mirroring.

I'm sure you've noticed that people engaged in an interesting conversation—they are excited about what they are saying
or what the other person is saying (in other words, they have
rapport)—always seem to take the same poses and make the
same movements. One leans forward and the other leans forward; one leans back and the other follows that lead. They cross
their hands in the same manner and at the same time, tilt their
heads simultaneously, seem to have similar side activities (he's
playing with his keychain, she's punching the end of her pen).

Their energy and concentration is on the conversation; everything else is happening subconsciously. Their minds are making a connection with each other, and their bodies are acting it out. This similarity not only creates a bond, it creates a feeling of ease, comfort, understanding and safety. You are together, mentally and physically.

Isn't it obvious this is exactly what you want the woman to feel? By mirroring her, I can subconsciously make her feel all these wonderful feelings about me, and I can develop instant rapport without lifting a finger (unless she lifts a finger and I mirror her).

I use three levels of mirroring. Once I get to the third level, I know I am in total control of the seduction situation.

1.  I begin with *following*, or doing the movement after she does it, including body position, hand motions, and facial expressions. I know what you're thinking: This is crazy! I'm going to get caught! She must see me copying her! Guess what: women never fully notice! They just sense it subconsciously and become more comfortable, relaxed, and (eventually) drawn to me.

2.  Then I start *pacing*, or doing the movements at the same time she does them. Sounds impossible, right? It isn't. In fact, since I've been following her and creating rapport, I will begin to pace her almost automatically. Our minds are picking up the stimuli from each other so fast that we are almost moving in tandem. Pretty great, huh? It gets even better.

3.  Once I've developed pace, I start *leading*, or having her imitate my movements. I usually wait for an important moment in the conversation—in this case, when I describe skiing to her—and begin to make intentional movements that she will subconsciously follow. The first time this happens to you, it will blow you away. You are getting

her to imitate you, controlling her subconscious mind without her even knowing it! Cough and she coughs. Scratch and she scratches. Because you're aware of the mirroring and putting effort into achieving it, your conscious mind is gaining the upper hand on her subconscious mind. Usually, physical leading keeps pace with my verbal leading—as she gives in to the power of my voice and words, she gives in to the movements of my body as well. But sometimes physical mirroring takes the lead, drawing the woman in subconsciously before her conscious mind has given itself over.

Mirroring is not easy, and many a developing seduction has gone off track because the guy focused too much on mirroring and forgot about the conversation. If you find mirroring difficult, forget it for now. Focus on demonstrating value and personality, and this more advanced technique will follow.

# Get Past No

I introduce a fictitious non-threatening female friend (see, I'm a sensitive guy!), cement the positive experience in her mind, and relate it to the experience we are currently sharing.

Let's remember where we left off, with me talking about skiing and saying, "You can feel your heart rate speeding up and the tingle all over your body. I just absolutely love that feeling, don't you?"

Ninety-eight percent of the time she will go along with this, because that really is the way she feels, but let's assume she says, "Not really."

There are two explanations for this, and neither is very promising. The first is that she honestly doesn't know what I'm talking about, which means she's probably either unimaginative or stupid. That doesn't disqualify her, but it's a major disappointment. Smart, adventurous women are better than dull, uninspired ones any day.

The second explanation, and the more likely one, is that she's blowing me off. That's strange, because up until now the conversation was going well. What happened?

I upped the ante. Consciously, or more likely subconsciously, she somehow made the connection to sex. Most people enjoy such connections as long as they think nobody else knows they made such a connection in their mind, but in this case for some reason she's self-conscious for having made that connection and is putting on the brakes.

So what to do? Should I try to get her to admit to the feelings? No! Never argue with a woman or make it seem like she's given a wrong answer.

Instead, I switch to the third person, introducing a fictitious non-threatening female friend (see, I'm a sensitive guy!), cement the positive experience in her mind, and relate it to the experience we are currently sharing. As always, I end with a question she has to answer.

"Well, I guess different people have different experiences. My friend Barbara just got back from skiing and told me that's exactly how she felt. So what makes you feel excited and happy?"

STEP **37**

# Touch Her

Words are a powerful tool, but there's something
even more powerful that is always at your
disposal: touch. Whenever you are in a seduction
situation, you should touch the woman in a
nonthreatening manner as often as possible.

Now let me make something perfectly clear: I am talking about
nonsexual, nonthreatening touching. Never grope a girl, "accidentally" touch her ass, or force yourself on her. That's not only
gross and demeaning, it borders on criminal.

With touching, my goal is not to "get a piece," but to simply
reinforce my connection with some good old-fashioned physical
contact. Psychological studies show that casual touching during
a friendly conversation causes people to remember the conversation more fondly, so I get to touching—and I don't waste any
opportunities.

Since we're sitting together, I go with the easiest kino to pull
off and accidentally rub my leg on hers. I leave it there just a moment longer than usual, then pull away. As the conversation
goes on, I'll go back to this move several times, perhaps even
commenting on how I keep bumping her if it seems appropriate.

This foot tomfoolery may amount to nothing, but it may also turn into a genuine flirtation. Often, a woman's first deliberate sign of interest is answering foot kino right back. In her mind, it's secret, hidden, easily dismissed as an accident, and therefore safe.

Additionally I waste no chances to put my hand on her wrist for a moment when I reassure her or share a secret with her, or pat her on her shoulder or back when I compliment her on either some real achievement, or better yet, I pull the "ironic pat on the back" in response to some blunder she either revealed in her conversation or committed as we were talking.

# Drop an Anchor

> Once I've touched her in the same way three
> times, I've set an anchor. Now when I touch her
> there again in the same way—with the same
> pressure and with the same motion—I will
> suddenly and unexpectedly evoke in her the
> feeling of happiness and excitement that she
> experienced when I planted the anchor.

Anchoring is based on the Pavlovian response, a reflex first explored and made famous by the Russian scientist Pavlov. In his experiment, Pavlov rang a bell and at the same time offered a dog some food. When he saw and smelled the food, the dog started to salivate. Pavlov repeated this many times over a period of days, always getting the dog to salivate at the sight and smell of the food. Then he rang the bell without offering the dog any food. As soon as he heard the bell, the dog started salivating. Pavlov had programmed a conditioned response, which would create the positive reaction even when the object of desire wasn't offered!

As you might already have guessed, this response works with people as well. My goal is to get this girl salivating at the thought of me. I want to keep her on a constant high, laughing and feeling great about herself (and by extension, me), but even for the most experienced pros that's easier said than done.

That's where anchoring comes in. I want to create a positive Pavlovian response, even when there's no apparent reason for her to feel happy. But how do I ring the bell?

Easy. The first time I see the girl really light up with delight—smiling, laughing, feeling good because of the positive feelings I have created for her—I touch her *in a specific place*. I usually go for the hand for the first anchor because it is usually available and easy to touch. If not, the elbow or the shoulder are also good.

When I touch her, I say, "It's a great feeling, isn't it?" or "Isn't that great?" This distracts her from my touch, which is important because I want her to feel it subconsciously. It also reinforces the physical anchor with a verbal anchor. She was feeling good, then I said she was feeling good, so something must feel great! But what is it? She doesn't know, but she knows she likes it!

Once I've touched her in the same way three times, I've set an anchor. Now when I touch her there again in the same way, with the same pressure and with the same motion, I will suddenly and unexpectedly evoke in her the feeling of happiness and excitement that she experienced when I planted the anchor. In other words, I rang the bell and suddenly she's salivating.

I usually try to plant three anchors: one on her hand; one on her back, elbow, or shoulder; and one (which is more sexual) on her knee. I try to establish them as early as possible. For one thing, it's always a good idea to touch her. For another, it takes about three touches to plant an anchor (or nine touches total for my three anchors). Why wait? Finally, momentum is often very strong in the beginning of a conversation. All conversations flag at some point, so I plant anchors early in anticipation of firing them off later and bringing her right back where I want her to be.

But be careful! Don't overuse your anchors because you will eventually desensitize her to them. Ring the bell ten times without food, and the dog will stop salivating. I only use my anchors two or three times without replanting them with more actual feelings of happiness—or horniness.

# Echo Her

All girls want to be understood. In order for my companion to feel understood, I not only listen to what she says, but spoon-feed it back to her in bite-sized chunks. Yes, it helps if I agree with her, but it's not always even necessary.

So when she answers my question about what makes her excited with "I collect antique dolls," do I say, "Yes, I completely agree. I love that, too!"?

Of course not. For one thing, it's obviously not true. No straight man worth sleeping with collects or cares about antique dolls. And even if it was possibly true—for instance, had she said she was really into yoga (kinky!)—I don't want to be so simplistic and obvious.

Instead, what I'm going to do is take what she said, paraphrase it, and present it as an original thought or opinion a few minutes later. With the dolls, I could go in a couple possible directions. I could go with a parallel hobby I hope she identifies with:

"I've always been really into stamp collection. A lot of people think that's stupid, but I love the hunt. I get really excited when I find something I really like. And it's great to spend time with something I care about, even if many other people don't share a similar passion." Obviously, I'm hoping she feels the same way about her dolls. If so, I've not only created kinship and mutual interest, but I've associated myself with a lot of important ideas—yes, her doll collection, but also excitement, the hunt, finding something she really likes, and not caring what other people think.

Or I can feed the information back to her more directly:

"I love people who collect things. They're very caring and thoughtful, but they're also passionate. They get excited when they find something they like, and they don't care if some people don't understand that."

I'm riffing on her original information, making it sound different, but still portraying the same attitude. Often, she won't remember she had previously said essentially the same thing and therefore, *bam*, she "realizes" we have so much in common that surely I'm the man of her dreams. Even if she's not immediately floored by this, I've shown her that I'm listening to and understanding her.

This kind of echoing is useful all the time, but it really comes in handy when you've elicited her values, which is what we're going to move on to next.

# The Fourth Stage

> Are you seeing a pattern here? That's right, there
> are a lot of phases, but you don't want to dwell on
> any of them longer than you have to.

All right, now we're moving to the fourth stage of seduction:
eliciting values. What's that? You're wondering what exactly the
other stages are? Okay, let's review.

1. *The opener.* You have to get her talking. You want to keep
   this as short as possible.
2. *Fluff talk.* Keep her talking, block the obstacles, and find a
   subject to talk about. You want to keep this as short as
   possible.
3. *The conversation.* You're focusing on positive emotions
   and feelings, not facts, to build rapport and positive associations. You want to keep this as short as possible.
4. *Eliciting values.* You're finding out what she wants in a
   man, and becoming that man for her. You want to keep
   this as short as possible.

Are you seeing a pattern here? That's right, there are a lot of phases, but you don't want to dwell on any of them longer than you have to. Don't rush, but always keep in mind these are not ultimate goals; they are steps on the way to the ultimate goal.

If you're getting tired of all this talking, keep your shirt on. Seduction is a process, and like all adventures the pleasure is in the journey as much as the destination.

And don't worry, we're almost there. There is only one step after eliciting values: the close.

# Elicit Her Values

> "Eliciting values" means finding out what she
> wants in a man and then turning into the man of
> her dreams by providing it for her. The secret is
> not to be the dream man, but *her* dream man.

"Eliciting values" means finding out what she wants in a man and then turning into the man of her dreams by providing it for her.

Think of it this way: You're a salesman. You're selling yourself. You don't want to use a generic pitch about how great the product is; that's not going to work. You need to find out what the customer wants and then show how that product will deliver on her needs.

The secret, in other words, is not to be *the* dream man, but *her* dream man.

Women like to feel that they're unique, that they have something you don't see in other women, and that's what makes them attractive to you. I create this feeling by focusing on her and asking her deep, meaningful questions that really probe her life and thoughts.

And I always pay attention when she's talking; I don't let

my thoughts wander to that delicious steak I had for dinner or the extraordinary perkiness of her breasts. This is critical because, in a few minutes, I'm going to feed those values back to her and show her how I fulfill them all.

I only know one foolproof way (and we're all fools sometimes) to elicit values, and that is to ask. We're laughing and talking and eventually, when there's a lull in the conversation, I lean in and ask, "If I were to ask you what's important to you in a relationship, what would you say?"

"I don't know."

"What kind of guys have you dated in the past?"

"I've always dated tall guys."

"Well, I'm not very tall, and obviously you've noticed that, so I guess you're not interested in me."

Wrong. Wrong. And wrong. That is a classic failure of imagination. What she just gave me was a "means value," in other words, a physical characteristic. It's not height that she's after, it's the *feeling* a tall man gives her when he's by her side. The same is true for good looks. She just wants the *feeling* a good-looking guy provides, which is why good looks aren't the only quality that matters, or even an important quality. Physical characteristics are only means values, so don't go out and get leg implants if you're short or rob a bank to become financially secure.

The important knowledge is not what she says she wants; it's the feeling she experiences when she is around those guys she describes. That's what I'm after, because that's what she's after.

STEP **42**

# Tackle the Second Blocker

As with the "Are you trying to seduce me?" block, she's reacting to the fact that (consciously or subconsciously) you're moving to the next level and taking her someplace she may not be quite comfortable going . . . yet. That is what seduction is about—taking a woman to the next level of intimacy, making her comfortable, then moving on to the next level, repeating the process up until that ultimate level of intimacy.

The target just told me she always ends up dating tall guys, so I nod (a subconscious, positive signal that creates rapport) and say, "And what do you experience when you're with a tall guy?"

Now instead of answering, she asks, "What's with the twenty questions all of a sudden?"

Nothing to worry about, though. This can happen if you seem to come up with questions way too conveniently instead of having them present themselves seemingly within the natural flow of the conversation. As long as she says it with a smile, it means she isn't really that committed to blocking you and just got a bit curious. Or it could also be that she simply isn't used to digging that deeply into her feelings and she needs a moment to think about it.

Or, as with the "Are you trying to seduce me?" block, she may also be reacting to the fact that you're moving to the next level and taking her someplace she's not quite comfortable going . . . yet. Of course, that is what seduction is about—taking a woman to the next level of intimacy, making her comfortable, then moving on to the next level again and again and again until . . . well, you know where this all ends up.

So what do I do when she throws up the Twenty Questions blocker?

I'm honest. No, I don't tell her I'm eliciting values because I'm trying to pick her up. I tell her what I'm really doing: trying to learn more about her so I can find out whether she is the type of person I should get to know even better. There's no way she can argue with that logic, right?

Then I run some positive reinforcement on her feelings. I say, "I enjoy getting to know women who are intelligent, caring, and open emotionally. It's wonderful to feel close to a woman like that."

Bingo! I've used what could have been a blocker as an opportunity to get that much closer to the ultimate goal.

STEP **4 3**

# Get Her to Explain Her Values

I've deflected the blocker, but I still need to elicit those values. So I head right back to my earlier question. "I'm still curious. What do you like about tall guys?"

"I don't know. I guess they just make me feel comfortable."

Bam! I've just moved from a means value with no seductive power to what she wants to feel like or her desired state. She wants to feel comfortable, and I already suspect that comfort comes from the actual end value she wants from this guy: security.

So I file away comfortable and ask her, "In what way does a tall guy make you feel more comfortable?"

"I don't know. I guess it's the fact that I feel I can rely on him. He's there when I need protection and I feel like I'm always protected when he's around."

Bingo! I just confirmed her end value—security. This is what she really wants from this guy and not that he be tall—height is just one of a number of means values that can give her the sense of security she needs. Now is also the perfect time to comment on her values, agree with them, and give your own "neutral" perspective.

"I know what you mean. Being able to protect my loved ones is the number one reason I took up self-defense / became a third-degree black belt in tae-kwon-do / spar regularly in my local mixed martial arts gym / went through the rigorous counterterrorist training offered by my company and graduated top of my office," etc. Just come up with something that actually applies to you. "I need to know that I am able to protect and defend those I care about when the situation calls upon it and I can't imagine it any other way." Don't be surprised if there's a wet spot on her chair when she gets up to excuse herself for a moment to go the bathroom. Suddenly you've become one of those tall men she's always felt drawn to even if you're no taller than a midget.

Such end values are the key to unlocking a woman's heart . . . or unhooking her bra. The end value is what she truly desires in a man. As long as you can create those feelings in her, and she associates those feelings with you, you're on your way to becoming her dream man.

How many values do you need? The more the better, my friend, but once you've got three there's no need to struggle for more. After three, it's time to move on.

---

### The Secret Targets Game

Eliciting values isn't as easy as it sounds. It's not that hard either, but it can take some practice. Here's a fun game you can play with a woman in a club, bar, or other socially active setting if you're struggling to get the values conversations going. Like all gimmicks, I suggest you make this a fallback plan and not your first line of attack. Relying on gimmicks keeps you from practicing the true skills—listening to a woman, understanding her values, and then feeding them back to her—but they are useful for carrying you forward if nothing else comes to mind.

So if you're dying out there, try looking around the bar and telling her: "Okay, I just picked out a guy for you to marry, a guy to fuck, and a guy to kill. Do you want to know who I picked?" Now point out the guys and explain why you think she'd want to do each of the above. You'll both be talking about what she values (and hates) about guys in no time. Once you're done, she'll probably want to do the same for you, so let her!

STEP **44**

# The Questions

I just made eliciting values seem really easy, didn't I? Well guess what, it is. This is one of the easiest steps because 1) you're already having a great conversation, and 2) all you're doing is asking her nonsexual (she thinks) questions about herself.

But it's not as easy as I made it seem; I just didn't want to try to write out three pages of realistic dialogue. It usually takes four or five questions to get from a means value to an end value.

And easy doesn't mean there aren't problems you could encounter here, and I'm not just talking about the "What's with all the questions?' block.

One common obstacle is that you're having a great conversation, but you can't get it to come around to the right subjects: her thoughts, feelings, and values. This only occurs, of course, when you've hooked a talker (see Step Fifteen if you've forgotten the difference between talkers and listeners). Talkers are great, but sometimes it's hard to reel them in.

When that happens, I go with the direct approach. I act a little confused and say, "I understand what you're saying, but you've got to ask yourself: What is most important to you in (whatever she's talking about)?"

If she doesn't take the bait, I just rephrase the question. "Alright, let me ask you then: What's really important to you in . . . ?"

Another possible obstacle is that she has really heinous, disgusting opinions that you just don't agree with. Don't argue with her. If you don't want to bail on principle, then ask her to explain her reasoning. Say: "I hadn't thought of it that way. When did you first begin to think that way?" If she hesitates (she may think you're being a smart-ass), say, "Seriously, I'm very curious. What experience convinced you of that opinion?" Her answer will not only be something important to her, but also a key way to change her mind about anything.

Always remember to frame your questions in the right way by forcing her to give you a long answer. Don't ask, "Do you value excitement in your life?" Her answer is going to be one word: yes or no. And even if she says yes, you haven't gotten any closer to what makes her excited. It could be skydiving or it could be unicorns, you have no idea.

The correct question is "What excites you?"

---

### The Nine Things to Know

There are nine important questions to ask about the woman when eliciting values. Do *not* phrase them this way; as always, you must use open-ended questions. Those questions should be used to discover these nine end values. And no, you don't have to discover all nine! In most cases, three will do.

1. What does she want?
2. What does she like?
3. What does she think she needs?
4. What does she think she deserves?

5. What did she have before that she wishes she had now?
6. What did she have before that she really wants to avoid?
7. What scares her?
8. What makes her happy?
9. What makes her horny?

# Learn Her Trance Words

> The words she repeats often or puts particular emphasis on are her Trance Words. These are the words she thinks with and is most familiar with. By remembering them and subtly repeating them back to her, I am tapping directly into her subconscious mind.

While I'm eliciting values, I listen on a very close level to the actual words she's saying. The words she repeats often or puts particular emphasis on are her Trance Words. By remembering them and subtly repeating them back to her, I am tapping directly into her subconscious mind. She won't know why, but she'll feel like I completely understand her, that we're "on the same wavelength," or even sometimes that we're soul mates. What I do and say is much more likely to be understood and appreciated because I've bound her to me just by using a few of her favorite words.

In this case, I picked up on *comfortable*. It was the first meaningful word (after *tall*) she used when describing her ideal man. I repeated it back to her immediately, then I filed it away in my memory to use again a little later in the conversation. My plan is to use it three or four times—I don't overdo it, I just want to make sure it sticks in her mind.

So when the conversation flags, I can look around and say, "I like this place. It's very comfortable. That's one of the primary things I look for in a bar, a place where I can just relax and be comfortable with someone . . ."

Trance Words are an incredibly powerful tool. And they're incredibly easy to use, right? Actually, they take a little getting used to. When you're just starting out, all this listening and filing can throw off your rhythm and leave the conversation stalled. But once you learn to automatically recognize and record Trance Words, you'll find yourself making a connection so strong you won't even realize where it came from.

# STEP **4 6**

# Touch Her

By now you're probably thinking, "Hey, hasn't this already been covered somewhere before?" Yes, it has. More than once, even. But touching is just too important to brush over lightly, plus unlike talking, it can be hard to overcome for many. Neither is this really a specific step that you do at some point and then forget about. It has to be a lingering thing throughout the interaction and so to emphasize that, I will bring it up one more time.

Touching is a vital tool to reinforce positive feelings. Never neglect your anchors and your foot flirt. Mirror her body language and touch her whenever the opportunity arises. At some point, though, if I say something and she responds positively, I touch her lightly on the hand or arm and that no longer is just an anchor; it's a sexual advance—but a very subtle and intimate one. More important, I am reinforcing her positive feeling with a warm touch.

When the conversation is going well, I reach over and brush something out of her hair or off her shoulder (and no, something doesn't actually have to be there). If that works, I wait a few minutes and brush an eyelash off her cheek. These are very delicate, sensitive maneuvers that require a light, sensual touch. Even better, they're the kind of things people do for each other when they're intimate, so I'm reinforcing our bond.

The most important thing to remember about any kind of touching is to *pay attention to how she responds*. If she's comfortable with nonsexual touching, then gradually get more sexual and explicit. She will either follow you straight into a makeout session, or she will tell you to stop when the contact gets so intimate it makes her uncomfortable.

This girl, for instance, draws the line at the eyelash. This is a mixed signal. She's been positive up until now, so the chances are that she likes my touch, but feels I'm going too fast. In this case, I go back to basic nonsexual hand and arm touching. She doesn't tell me to stop, so we're back to our outer boundaries . . . for now.

Always remember that if a woman tells you to stop, by all means stop touching her and respect her space. Some women love to be touched; some women feel it's a serious invasion of their personal space. They may be very attracted to you, and love what you're saying, but are very private about being touched (until you're *in private,* that is). Always respect her feelings, and never force anything with touching.

STEP **47**

# Tell Her a Story

> Girls love to dream. My job now is to use
> her dreams to create intense emotions and
> links to me.

Here's where I put it all together. I've acquired the tools; now I'm going to build her a dream. I'm going to tell her a story that makes her feel like I am the special man for her. I'm going to use her values, her interests, and her Trance Words. I'm going to call in my anchors by touching her at the right time and in the right spot. I'm going to touch her again. And of course I'm going to use positive, open body language and look deep into her eyes.

Girls love to dream. My job now is to use her dreams to create intense emotions and links to me. To do that, I need to talk about her favorite fantasies, like walking hand in hand on the beach, or making out under a tropical waterfall. This is risqué sex talk, especially with a girl I just met, but she'll have little resistance to participating because it's all perfectly safe. After all, it's only a fantasy.

The key to linking this fantasy to me is time distortion. I'm not just describing a hypothetical event, I'm talking about something that is going to take place six months in the future—next spring, next summer, next winter, whenever is appropriate. And I'm not going to be in this fantasy alone, I'm going to be there with *that special someone*. The fact that she is that special someone will be obvious without me having to say it.

So let's review what I know. Keep in mind that in a real seduction scenario I'd know a lot more than this.

- She likes skiing.

- She likes antique dolls (but I have no knowledge or experience in this area).

- She values security.

- A Trance Word is *comfort*.

Now I create a fantasy to fit her values.

"I love traveling, and I'd love to go on a ski trip next year. If you had one place to choose to go skiing, where would it be?"

"Probably Colorado."

"I always feel comfortable in Colorado. Can't you just see yourself there? Skiing, the mountains, relaxing . . . What's your favorite part about skiing Colorado?"

"I love riding up in the ski lift. It's so beautiful and peaceful."

"It makes you feel warm, doesn't it? Even on a cold day. Especially if you have someone you feel comfortable with sitting beside you to share it. You can laugh and play with each other. That's fun, isn't it?"

As I was saying the last two sentences, I played the anchor I'd previously put on her wrist—the one for happiness. She's instantly flooded with positive emotions while thinking about riding the ski lift with . . . guess who? So now I shift into fantasy mode.

"How about you take a lodge as well? After a fun day on that ski trip, you'd sit by a warm fire, next to someone special, feeling the warmth spreading through your muscles, feeling the relaxation, feeling so comfortable and secure in each other's arms."

She says, "Do I get hot chocolate?"

Now I touch her on the anchor I've previously put on her inner elbow—the one for horniness. This is a very sensual spot, and while she won't feel my light touch on her skin, she'll definitely feel the change in her body.

"With marshmallows in it. And he could massage your shoulders, working his way slowly down your back, and then the two of you could slip into a warm, comfortable hot tub and feel the heat rising up all around you . . ."

When it works, man, time distortion is powerful. I've only known this girl ten minutes, but after a dip in the hot tub together (notice it was all implied; I let *her* make the connection) she feels like she's known me ten months. No need to go on and on making meaningless chit-chat now. It's time to close this encounter.

STEP **48**

# Analyze the Boyfriend Blocker

> My job isn't to psychoanalyze her; my job is to
> read her emotions and determine why she's
> bringing up the "borefriend" all of a sudden. There
> are three possible reasons she just put up the
> boyfriend blocker.

"You know, you're nice and everything, and I'm having a good time, but I've got a boyfriend."

Whoa! Where did that come from? I thought this was going well; now I guess the party is over.

Not so fast. The boyfriend isn't necessarily the end of the line. First of all, this is very deep into the conversation to be bringing up the boyfriend. She's obviously been enjoying flirting with me. Maybe she's mad at him. Maybe she's bored with him . . .

Whoa, hold on again, hombre. Why worry about all that? My job isn't to psychoanalyze her; my job is to read her emotions and determine why she's bringing up the "borefriend" all of a sudden. There are three possible reasons she just put up the boyfriend blocker.

1. *She's loyal to her man and enough is enough.* You can usually tell this pretty quickly because her whole demeanor will change. Specifically, she'll close up her posture and get suddenly serious. Basically, she's had fun, but she's not going any further. This is a great time to be a gentleman and bail.

2. *She is using the boyfriend to up the level of excitement.* She wants you; she's using him to add danger and turn you both on. This play is even more obvious than loyalty because she'll be flirty with it, laughing and pretending to pull away, then rush back to you with her kino and her eyes.

3. *She's wavering in her commitment.* Either she's feeling guilty because she's thinking of how great it would be to cheat on him just this once, or she's trying to throw up a last blocker because she's falling for you. If she tells you the truth, then she's off the hook, right?

My guess with this girl is that it's number three. She's not being flirty, and she definitely isn't walking away. If this were earlier in the conversation, I'd use one of three basic brush-offs, usually in this order.

First, *ignore it:*

"Sorry, I have a boyfriend."

"As I was saying, I really feel comfortable here . . ."

If she mentions him again, *humor it:*

"Sorry, I have a boyfriend."

"Hey, we just met. Don't start laying all your problems on me already."

Then *downplay it:*

> "I'm just kidding. I'm happy you have a boyfriend
> because I'm not looking for a girlfriend. I'm just looking
> for a girl I can talk to, really feel comfortable with . . ."

I'm well past that right now, though. I've already established that I'm interested in this girl—not just her body, but everything about her—and I don't want to lose that momentum now. I'm just going to have to take the time to smash the boyfriend. It's time to plant the seeds of doubt, then water them and see them grow.

STEP **49**

# Smash the Boyfriend

> I never insult the boyfriend. I never say outright, "I bet he's cheating on you." I always stand up for him and make "excuses" for his behavior. I'm not trying to break up the relationship; I'm on his side!

Every boyfriend blocker comes with a built-in opener: If she has a boyfriend, where is he? I'm going to throw a few seeds of doubt in there and see if I can get them to grow.

"Sorry, I have a boyfriend."

"And he's not here! I can't believe he'd let you out of his sight. Where is he?"

"He's out with his friends."

Perfect. Now I just have to create an image in her mind of him cheating on her. Whether he is or not, of course, is irrelevant. If I can get her to imagine that her boyfriend isn't entirely trustworthy, this alternative version of reality will eat away at her all night and wear her inhibitions down.

I never insult the boyfriend. I never say outright, "I bet he's cheating on you." I always stand up for him and make "excuses" for his behavior. I'm not trying to break up the relationship; I'm on his side! Meanwhile, I keep asking leading questions.

"Do his friends go out to bars?"

"I'm not really sure what they do. Guy stuff, I guess."

"Like pick up women?" She looks stunned. "Not him, of course, but his friends. Do his friends have as much luck picking up beautiful women as he does?" (Meaning her, of course, but also implying he's a ladies' man.)

"No, it's not like that."

"Oh. I always like to spend my evenings with beautiful women—whether I'm involved with them or not. It makes me feel happy and comfortable (Trance Word). I thought most men felt the same."

"Maybe that's because you're a gigolo."

It's okay; she's smiling, but the seed of doubt has been planted pretty deep. Now I water it with—what else?—a story about a friend.

"Reminds me of a recent situation with a friend of mine. Susan, this friend, didn't really mind that her boyfriend used to go out with the guys. After all, she was loyal to him, so what else could she have expected from her boyfriend as well, right? Well, wrong. Being a guy, he just couldn't resist the temptations of this apparent "freedom," and he probably wouldn't even have gotten caught, if all those other girls hadn't started sending raunchy text messages to his cellphone, which of course Susan discovered at some point. Needless to say, Susan felt really betrayed and cheated. The interesting thing is, or at least the way she told me this, had she known about it before, she would not have passed up a few opportunities herself. I'm not saying this has anything to do with our situation, but these things just happen you know."

Now I play down the whole boyfriend angle. After all, a boyfriend isn't forever, right?

"She probably should have dumped him a long time ago. He didn't really make her happy. Now she realizes she was wasting time, passing up great opportunities (yourself) because of some promise she made to someone who wasn't even there for her."

I throw in a bunch of my mythical friend's boyfriend's annoying habits, everything from he forgot to call her sometimes to he left his toothbrush all crusty every morning. How do I know I'm making progress? She starts mentioning things that are wrong with her boyfriend, even though they're trivial (Who cares if he cuts the crust off his bread?) and she's smiling and joking about them. She's not over him yet, but she's starting to open up.

Even better, she's starting to focus on the negatives. When she gives me a more serious complaint (like not calling her when he's out), I ask her some follow-up questions so that she has to really think about all the negative implications: Does she think he's cheating? Does he just not care that much? Is he unreliable? After all, this girl values security.

Finally, it's time to talk about ex-boyfriends. Did they treat her the same way? If I can get her to start talking about one ex-boyfriend in particular, I've done two very important things. First, she's thinking about a man other than her man. Second, she's realizing that boyfriends are temporary things and that the loyalty she feels now is just another version of a loyalty she felt in the past and eventually left behind. Clearly, she was wrong about the ex-boyfriend when they were going out and she feels much better since she left him. The implication: Leaving a boyfriend is a positive.

In this case, the ex she chooses to talk about was a great guy (surprisingly, this happens a lot), so I coax her along with memories of how passionate their lovemaking was and how horny he used to make her. Now I'm working the opposite angle. Not only will her current boyfriend pale in comparison, but I'm getting a free pass on some safe, guilt-free sex talk.

In fact, this girl's getting horny right now just thinking about her ex—hornier than she's been all night—so I start giving her a little kino: shoulder massage, back rub, hold her from behind, stuff she doesn't get every day from her absentee lover. She's going to want to release that pent-up passion somewhere, and it's time to make sure she releases it with me.

STEP **50**

# The Close

> The close is the moment where you extend an explicit invitation—or more accurately, get her to extend a specific invitation to you.

This is it. This is what you came for, the moment where you move this encounter from the merely conversational (no matter how hot and bothered) to the invitation. The faster you can get to this point, the better, as I've already pointed out plenty of times, so don't be shy about closing. Not closing is like taking three hours to shop for groceries and then leaving all the goodies you amassed in your shopping cart stranded in the middle of the supermarket and leaving without buying a thing.

The close is the moment where you extend an explicit invitation—or more accurately, get her to extend a specific invitation to you. There are two basic types of closes. You can think of them as now or later. Both closes are effective; it's the *situation* that tells you which one to use.

### The Two Basic Closes

1. *The Invitation Close* (now)—You're inviting her to leave with you right now.

2. *The Number Close* (later)—You're getting her to offer her
   phone number with an invitation to call her.

For the sake of instruction, I'm going to walk you through
both closes, starting with The Invitation Close. I know, I know,
I'm changing the style of the book, but the fact is this: The close
is simply too important to leave to your imagination.

STEP **51**

# Sex Talk

Some people may disagree with me, but I feel strongly that if you've got an opening for sex talk, you go for it. If you have calibrated the girl correctly, sex talk can take an encounter from ordinary to extraordinary in a few minutes, plus it's a ton of fun.

Remember, you never *start* a conversation with sex talk or sexual innuendo. Don't misunderstand me—the emphasis here is on the word *start*. First, you have to establish rapport, understand her values, echo them back to her. Notice her body language becoming more friendly and open. Drop a few anchors. Get positive feedback on the touching, preferably with reciprocal touching. Create the fantasy for her.

Now move on to sexual talk if—and this is a big if—you are planning to try the Invitation Close. In other words, if your goal is to take this girl home tonight, you need to try sex talk first and see how she responds.

But how?

There are two things to always remember in any seduction conversation, and they are especially true for sex talk.

1. Don't brag. Bragging makes you look like a loser.

2.  Use the friend. Tell her a story about your friend (and no, the friend doesn't have to be real), not about yourself or about her. This cushions the shock of frank sexual talk.

Remember those simple rules and it's easy. All you do is mention a sexual situation and watch her reaction.

In this case (remember, I left her at the ski lodge), I say, "My friend Kate once had sex with a stranger in a hot tub. (I laugh.) I know, that's kind of a forward revelation coming from a woman and all, but we're really good friends and for some reason she still mentions it from time to time, so I guess she really liked it."

Yes, it's bold, but remember, I'm only going to sex talk because she's been giving me signs and I plan to take her home (or at least out of the bar) in the next two minutes. I'm pushing the envelope, attempting to make her drop her inhibitions. That's why "the friend" is essential. I can safely talk about graphic sex and she can safely get horny because, after all, I'm not talking about me or her.

Most women will recoil slightly when you drop sex into the conversation for the first time. This is their gut reaction, and not necessarily a reflection of their true feelings. If you feel confident you're in the zone, as in, she's been giving you the signs, don't back off. Pursue the topic with no apologies, and she will usually spring back to a very positive reaction. This isn't true of all cases, but if you've calibrated the girl correctly, you should be able to see whether she's truly appalled by your dirty talk or merely hesitant but intrigued.

Sex talk is the perfect bridge from conversation to an invitation because it changes the dynamic of the relationship. Once you bring up sex, she will be forced to think about having sex with you. If she finds this a pleasant or intriguing idea, she will echo the sex talk back to you. Once you're engaged in sexual banter, even of the joking type, you are in. Move on to closing.

But be warned: Sexual banter does not necessarily mean that

she *wants* to have sex with you. She's just entertaining the thought, contemplating the idea, and first and foremost is only interested in pursuing the matter just a bit further, perhaps over a cup of coffee or in a phone conversation. So don't panic if she doesn't go for the Invitation Close; the game is still yours to win.

STEP **52**

# The Invitation Close

The Invitation Close is not an invitation to sex—at least not directly. The goal of the Invitation Close is to get her on a "date" right now.

In other words, your move is to suggest a change of venue where the two of you can get more comfortable. The key is simply to get her out of the current environment and into a place where you and she can be alone together. It doesn't matter if that place is crowded with strangers because none of these new people know you two just hooked up. They'll probably think you've known each other for months. This may not be important to you, but it's probably very important to her.

So where should you go? It's always better to have thought that out beforehand, which is why you should have five to seven standard choices you always use. Taking a walk is nice because it gives the two of you a chance to snuggle up and do some romantic making out, but you don't want to go for a walk on a busy street with garbage piled everywhere; that's going to kill the mood. And for heaven's sake, don't take her anywhere even remotely dangerous, such as an alley, or a dark and empty park. The chances are she'll be more worried you're a psycho than confident you're going to protect her from one.

What about the cheesy "Oh, my place is around the corner.

Do you want to come in?" Yes, it's cheesy, but it often works. Remember, she wouldn't be here if she wasn't at least *considering* the possibility of having sex with you at some point. But that word *considering* is important. You've still got to be sexy, romantic, and the man of her dreams, so talking about the neighborhood and why you like to live there (using her Trance Words, of course) is better than a cheesy invitation.

Another good option is going out for a coffee or a light snack. Obscure but romantic hole-in-the-wall kinds of places are perfect for this. Surprise her by taking her to a place she didn't even know existed, but that is cozy and warm, and has some delicious specialty to offer with which you can treat her senses. Look for a place that's quiet, private, soothing, romantically lit, and only a short walking distance from your apartment.

# What About the Friends?

Hold on there, hombre. The Invitation Close isn't that simple, especially in our scenario in which you've led a girl away from a group of friends. Before she leaves with you, every self-respecting woman is going to stop and say, "Wait, I can't just leave my friends here."

This is a momentum killer and it's very important that you keep the momentum moving forward. If her friends are close by or otherwise easily accessible (for example, via the phone), let her deliver the quick message. But if it looks like she either won't be able to find her friends that easily or that she could get stuck with them, say "Don't worry. We haven't seen them for ages, so they're probably having a good time. Plus, we can come back anytime and be gone for only a moment if you're worried, and they won't even notice that we were gone." Then take her hand, lead her to the door, and jump in the nearest cab.

STEP **54**

# The Invitation Close vs. the Number Close

> Remember one of the most important rules of seduction: Always leave at a high point in the conversation.

What's wrong with the Invitation Close? Seems like the stuff, doesn't it? Well, yes, when it works, it's magic, but there's one very important thing wrong with it: This close takes a long time.

Remember one of the most important rules of seduction: always leave at a high point in the conversation. The corollary to this rule is: As soon as the woman wants you, leave.

But that isn't what happens with the Invitation Close, is it? With the Invitation Close, as soon as she wants you, you proceed with sex talk. Then you try to get her horny. Then you invite her out with you.

In order for you to close her, she has to be willing to walk out of the bar with a guy she just met. In front of her friends, and a room full of people who (in her mind) are watching and judging her.

Don't worry, if you've calibrated her right, she'll come anyway. Women leave bars with strange men more often than you think. Still, it's a pretty hazardous obstacle. For many women, there is a public life and a sex life and never the two shall meet. In other words, they want to have casual sex, but they don't want other people to know about it.

Almost every girl, even the good girls, has at least a few wild flings in her life where she throws caution and common sense to the wind and just goes for it. Sex talk plus an invitation will make that happen—and why shouldn't that magical night happen with you?

Even if this sounds like a long shot, it really isn't. As long as she seems to be going along with it and feels comfortable, by all means, do proceed.

However, depending on the circumstances, proceeding may not always be a viable option and here's where the Number Close comes into play.

STEP **5 5**

# The Number Close

> The object of every seduction situation is to get
> her phone number and a promise to meet again.
> Notice, this is a two-part objective: Get her phone
> number *and* a promise to meet again.

Closing isn't about having sex right now. Often, seduction doesn't
work that way. The object of every seduction situation is to get
her phone number and a promise to meet again. Notice, this is a
two-part objective: Get her phone number *and* a promise to meet
again.

Every time I leave a woman, unless I've decided to bail (and
there's no shame in that, my friend!), I close her. Even if I'm
planning to come back and talk to her in fifteen minutes (after
that brisk walk around the block that makes me look busy), I extract a phone number and a promise to meet again. What if she
suddenly has to leave? Never take that risk, especially if she's
with friends. Get that number.

The best way to do this is to simply tell her to give it to you
like it's the most natural thing in the world. You don't *ask* for her
phone number, because even though things have been progress-
ing well, why on earth would you risk stalling things by actually

giving her a choice? Nope. Instead, say something like "Oh my God. I was having such a good time (Play that anchor!) talking to you that I didn't realize what time it was. I've got to go. Why don't you give me your phone number so we can continue this conversation at some later point."

You see, when given a choice, people will need to start thinking. Since they are expected to make a choice and a value judgment, they will need to start thinking about the pros and cons and the goods and bads of this and that, and that can all be very tiring. On the other hand, people tend to do what they're told ("Give me your number . . ."), especially when they're given a good reason to go along with it (". . . so that we can continue this conversation").

Instead of saying "Um, I don't know, its been nice, but I kinda have a boyfriend," she'll now go "Yeah, sure, of course, here it is."

Sounds good? Well, believe it or not, there's even a better way to get a phone number—to get her to offer it herself.

STEP **56**

# The Number Close: An Even Better Way

So what's the idea behind the Number Close? Simple. My objective is to get her number, but make it seem like it was *her* idea to give it to me. This way I'm leaving her with the thought "I gave him my number . . . I must like him," as opposed to the standard "He prompted me for my number . . . he must like me."

In the first situation, she's the one with the desire so I've got the power; in the second, I'm just another guy trying to pick her up. So instead of prompting her to give you her number, I look at my watch (or check the time on my BlackBerry, or with her, etc.) and tell her, "Oh my God. I was having such a good time (Play that anchor!) that I didn't realize what time it was. I've got to go. But I'd love to get together and go rollerblading sometime."

Whoa! Where did that come from? Actually, it came from the very start of the conversation, back in Step Thirty-four (go ahead, double-check). You may not remember that she mentioned it, but I do, because I'm making an effort to remember everything.

The best thing about rollerblading is that she probably doesn't remember she's mentioned it either. It's not like we'd been talking about it, but then wow! Somehow I happened to choose something she enjoys. We must really be soul mates!

There are two general rules I've observed that makes this tactic successful. First, I suggested something specific. If she gives me her number now, it's with the mutual understanding that we're going to meet later.

Second, rollerblading is not a date. Honestly, you don't want to go on a "date" with a woman unless the two of you are really dating. Going on a date with someone you're not actually dating looks quite desperate and it just puts unnecessary pressure on the encounter. You don't want her saying, "Do I want to go on a date with this guy?" You want her saying, "What's the harm in hanging out for a while?"

So never invite a girl you don't even know yet to dinner in a restaurant or a movie. At the restaurant you'd be expected to pay (since it was your idea, after all) and there are not many things worse than starting off any kind of relationship with a woman by paying for her. At the movies you'll hardly be able to get to know each other better or amplify the attraction since you're just sitting in silence and staring at the screen. Even worse, what if the movie is a bore? You'd certainly be associated with the same feelings then and let me assure you, boredom is not a feeling that will make a woman want to have sex with you.

If you can't think of anything and you didn't pick up a casual activity she's interested in during the conversation either, taking her for coffee near her home or office will fit the bill.

When I approach the situation this way, I anticipate her saying, "Sure. Here's my number."

But she doesn't bite. She just says, "That sounds like fun." Hmmm. What do I do now? Okay, I'll try to coax it out of her. There's a two-part trick I usually use here, both ends of which involve me playing forgetful. Why? Because if this works, I leave the encounter with her chasing me. Does that matter? You bet it does, because that's exactly how she's going to remember the encounter tomorrow. She's going to remember that she wanted me to call her.

Once I get the response that she's interested, I pick up my coat (if I have one) and say, "Great. I'll call you tomorrow."

Hopefully, she says, "But you don't have my phone number!"

But she doesn't. She's a sneaky one—or possibly inexperienced.

Now I walk away about five paces, stop and stand still (on the assumption she's watching me), then turn around and come back to the table. I smile and say, "You know what? If we ever want to do this again, laugh and have a good time, we need to know how to get hold of each other. What do you figure we should do about that?"

It's pretty obvious at this point what she needs to do now. Most of the time, the girl says, "Oh my God, I forgot to give you my phone number!" You'll be amazed how often they genuinely forget.

STEP **57**

# Tackling the Blockers in the Number Close

> The response is simple if she asks for your number:
> *Don't* give it to her.

There are two basic blockers for the Number Close. They're big, they're a little scary, and they're always hanging around, but they're also easy to outsmart. Unless she's giving you the complete blow-off, in which case you really screwed up early in the meeting and completely missed her signs, there is absolutely no reason to be thrown by the closer blockers.

## Blocker #1: She refuses.

If she seems reluctant to give you her phone number, it may be that she is simply overwhelmed. This happens, especially if you try to go straight from the approach to the close. Whatever you do, don't ask for the number again or pester her into giving it to you. This makes you look desperate and makes her suspicious of your motives. Play it cool. Remain polite and calm, like it's no big deal.

But remember that persistence pays. Stay in there and drop back into eliciting values. It's time to circle back around and give yourself another chance.

I can hear you now: "But I just used the appointment excuse!" Well, now you're on the clock. You've only got about five more minutes to win her over, but if you're feeling good about the direction of the conversation and you've calibrated this girl well, five minutes should be more than enough. Don't panic. Nobody gets called out for one strike.

## Blocker #2: She asks for your number instead.

I walk back to this girl and say, "You know what? If we ever want to do this again, laugh and have a good time, we need to know how to get hold of each other. What do you figure we should do about that?"

And she says, "Oh cool, why don't you give me your phone number?"

The response is simple if she asks for your number: *Don't* give it to her. Many women are collectors—they like to get phone numbers, but they have no intention of using them. Some even have a little competition with their friends to see who can get the most numbers in a week or month. Is this girl looking at me as just another sucker for her unused Rolodex?

I don't think this would be the case with this girl, though. For some reason she's just uncomfortable giving out her number to a virtual stranger, and that reason is probably that she has a boyfriend. It doesn't matter. I'm going to act like she's just a tease anyway.

"I really thought we had something special. But now it feels like you're just a naughty girl playing a naughty-girl game to collect numbers and impress her friends."

If she is just playing games, I've showed her that I'm not just another chump and earned her respect. But that's not the case here, because she quickly says, "No, no. I'm not that kind of girl . . ."

"There's only one way to convince me of that."

This girl likes me, there's no doubt about that. How many chances can I give her to give me her number?

Now she's got a serious look on her face, and I know what she's thinking before she even says it: She wants to see me again, but she really, really doesn't want me to call her. Maybe she lives with her parents. Maybe her roommate is a good Catholic pulling her moral strings. Maybe she lives with her boyfriend or . . . her husband. (In which case, it's worth a try to get her to your place right now. No time like the present when it's an affair of the . . . let's call it the heart.)

Or maybe she just doesn't have a cell phone? Unlikely, but you could still throw a joke about the state of the economy and how it affects the ordinary people so that not everyone can even afford a phone and how you really feel for her.

But as for getting the number, this is not the time to be aggressive. Some women, for whatever reason, like their privacy. Don't harass her for a number. That just makes you seem desperate, jerky, or a little bit scary. Instead, try to take her home right now.

# Closing the Number Close

> I always give the girl a specific time that I am
> going to call her. I look at the number (Does it
> have seven digits? Does it look fishy?) and say,
> "Great. I'll call you tomorrow around five. Is that
> a good time for you?"

This is extremely important: Whether I get her number (which is mostly what happens and thus should also happen to you) or let her off the hook because there's obviously issues at home, I never just tell her, "Great. Thanks. I'll call you sometime," or even "I'll be calling you soon."

I always give the girl a specific time that I am going to call her. I look at the number (Does it have seven digits? Does it look fishy?) and say, "Great. I'll call you tomorrow around five. Is that a good time for you?"

If possible (and why wouldn't it be, it's just a phone call), I always set up the call for the next day. There really is no science in "How long do I wait before I call her?" Just call her the next day and that's it. If you had a good thing going, why would you wait two or three days for her good memories to fade? Those trying to play hard to get by not calling until a specific number of days have passed are fooling nobody but themselves. I'm not being desperate by calling her the next day. I'm just a man who knows what he wants and isn't afraid to go after it. Besides I told her right away I'd be calling the next day, so neither is it like I simply couldn't contain myself—I'm just a strong, driven man, who has his life under control and well organized. Even if that's not the truth, that's what you want her to think.

Next, I always leave her with a suggestion that romance is in the future. In this case: "I'm sure we'll come up with more fun ideas for things to do when rollerblading. I can't wait." I've planted the idea, but I haven't come on too strong or needy.

Finally, I use a few lines to soften her up for the phone call. "Listen, I've got a fun suggestion. When I call you, I don't want you to answer, 'Huh? Who? Oh yeah . . . so how's it goin'?' That's just boring. I've got a better idea—when I call, I want you to act really enthusiastic and happy, like, 'You called! God, I'm so glad.' Okay? Does that sound like fun? Do we have a deal?"

I say it as if I'm joking (kind of), with a big smile. This ends the exchange on a light, friendly, and positive note, which almost automatically kick-starts the phone call from the same place. In fact, many girls repeat the answer I suggested back to me. They're joking, but those positive qualities are still on their minds.

# The Kiss

> Do not expect her to come right out and ask
> for a kiss. We all wish it were that easy, but that's
> just not the way it goes. *It's your duty to make
> the move*, so lean in and give her the kiss that
> will keep her wanting more.

You should always follow up the Number Close with an attempt to kiss her. Usually, I can tell from her body language that she is ready and waiting for the good-bye kiss. She will let me touch her without resistance and touch me in return; she will wet her lips or look at my lips. These are subconscious signals of desire. Read them and take advantage of them.

Do not expect her to come right out and ask for a kiss. We all wish it were that easy, but that's just not the way it goes. *It's your duty to make the move,* so lean in and give her the kiss that will keep her wanting more. If she seems receptive, I try to give her an open-mouthed kiss. If her body language is a little more closed, I stick to a closed-mouth kiss, but try to make it last a few seconds.

Of course, you have to be smart about the situation. If she's with her family, don't try the Kiss Close. Even if she wants to kiss you, the situation is awkward, especially if you've just met. The same can sometimes be true if her friends are standing right there. That's why it's always best to extract her from the group.

In all other cases, however, you *must* go for the Kiss Close. Don't ever ask, "Can I kiss you?" That old line puts her on a pedestal from which it becomes way too easy to reject you. And once again, why would you want her to be making the choices. Just take responsibility and go for it. The chances are very high she'll kiss you back, at least for a few seconds. If she pulls away, don't force it. Do exactly what you'd do if she'd just given you a full-on tongue down: smile and walk away.

With the kiss, the encounter is over. I usually get up, leave the bar, and do something useful with the rest of my night. But this seduction is far from having run its course. After all, we haven't done anything yet.

# The Phone Call

First, successful guys don't ask, they recommend. Second, movies, museums, and dinners out are for girlfriends they're already sleeping with.

There's no breaking the golden rule: Call her when you said you were going to call her, the very next day at a specific time. Yes, you can be five or even ten minutes late—it heightens the anticipation, right?—but don't make too much of a game out of this because it doesn't really matter. It's more important to remember what this phone call is about: setting up a time to meet her again.

Most pick-up gurus agree that a long phone conversation is the kiss of death. You want to do your seduction in person, not from across town, so always get right to the point during the follow-up phone call. The best way to do this is to say you're very busy and only have a minute to talk, but you don't want to miss the opportunity to be with her again.

So now what—do you ask her on a date?

Nope. First, successful men don't ask, they recommend. Second, movies, museums, and dinners out are for girlfriends they're already sleeping with.

In most cases, I should already have the casual encounter set up. Remember, I invited this girl rollerblading last night. So what do I say now?

"Hi, it's Tony."

"You called! God, I'm so glad."

"(Laugh.) I see you were paying attention and you also have a good memory. I like that. Look, it's really busy over here, but I didn't want to miss the opportunity to talk to you again. So we had rollerblading in mind, right? How about Wednesday evening at the park—does that sound good?"

I've kept it quick, casual, and specific. I've made it perfectly clear this is not a date without saying this directly. The activity is part of it, but equally important is suggesting a meeting in the middle of the week. The weekend, especially at night, always seems like a date, no matter how casual you try to make the get-together. If I asked her out for the weekend, I'd send all kinds of wrong messages: that I don't have anything to do on the weekend already; that I'm arranging my schedule around her; that I'm already getting serious. Instead, I've turned a boring Wednesday into a casual encounter with a mysterious man.

"I'm busy Wednesday."

"Okay, my Thursday schedule is full, but I think I could squeeze it in later that evening."

"Well, Thursday after work is hard for me."

"Okay, then, I'll tell you what. We both seem to be kind of busy, but why don't we meet for a cup of coffee and some stimulating conversation near your office during lunch or right after work. How's that work for you?"

"Um, well, I don't know . . ."

If she says she's busy, that's fine. We live in a busy world and women are busy, too. Try another time. If that doesn't work, I switch tactics to an even simpler get-together and coffee near a woman's office, which usually works best. If she still says no, she's obviously developed some second thoughts, but you have nothing to lose, so just tell it like it is.

"Wow, we had such a fun time last night and it seemed like we really hit it off so well. But now it's like it never happened and I'm just wasting my time here. I mean, we did have a great time didn't we? Or am I just dreaming?" Your goal is to pace her reality so she sees how rude she is being, and what an opportunity she is missing. At worst, you want to convince her that it's completely inconsiderate not to meet with you after all you've been through together. No, it's not the ideal way to get a girl out in private with you, but it's better than having everything fall apart over the phone. Once you're sitting with her again, you'll have another chance to remind her what she liked about you in the first place.

---

### Crib Notes

The phone call should be brief and to the point, but keep the techniques that you've learned so far, such as eliciting values, in mind. It's a little more difficult to elicit values over the phone than in person, especially if you're just starting out, but this is nicely counter-balanced by another advantage the phone gives you. She can't see you, so before you call, write down a few seductive lines of questioning and conversation topics, then simply consult the list if the need arises. Write down her Trance Words and values, too. Now it's as easy as reading those words and values back to her. Just make sure your delivery is natural; reading from a script will get you nowhere.

# The "You Probably Ask Girls Out All the Time" Block

One reason to confront the girl over the phone is because she might tell you why she is hesitating. In this case, the girl gives me a pretty classic response. "I don't know. You probably ask girls out all the time." This is a common variant of the even more direct "You seem like a player."

What happened? Maybe she's had some time to think about me and got scared, either of her feelings or of my charm; more likely, her girlfriends got to her after I left the bar. Someone with no experience with this might panic and lie, but . . .

When she asks if I go out with a lot of women, I don't lie. This isn't a bad thing for her to know. In fact, some PUAs intentionally drop into their suggestion of a meeting the fact that meeting women isn't new to them. They'll begin the invitation with something like: "I've taken women to some of the nicest restaurants and theaters in town, and it's been great. But I've also been with women when all we did was drink coffee, and I've liked that even more. It all depends on whether you need the scenery for support, and I'm betting we don't. So let's just make this casual and get a coffee tomorrow."

As long as it doesn't sound like bullshit or bragging, this approach gives you power. It lets her know you get around and lots of other women find you desirable. It shows her that meeting a woman for coffee isn't a big deal for you, which takes the pressure off and puts her at ease. You're also planting the idea that you're not suggesting a coffee meeting because you're cheap; you're suggesting it because it's the perfect way to get to know her better without distractions. How can she argue with that? She can't—and neither can she suggest a meal instead now without sounding greedy and shallow.

The danger is that you may lead the woman to think that she's not important to you; that you're the type of guy who dates around for sport. Obviously, this can end any relationship prematurely, so if she asks whether I date often, I play it a little more conservative.

"Yes, I do go out with a lot of girls. Because I'm picky."

"That doesn't sound picky."

"I'm waiting for the perfect girl. Someone I can talk to and feel comfortable (her Trance Word) with. Is it better if I stay home alone, hoping she shows up, or go out and search for her?"

By framing the question this way, I've forced her to respond. Any reasonable girl will have to admit that I'm right—sitting around alone waiting is stupid, for both me *and* her.

"Okay, let's get coffee at six on Wednesday." (Yes, she clearly lied about being busy earlier, but who cares? I've won her over for now.)

"Great. How about the place on Park."

"That's a little far from my office. How about the other place on Rose."

"I'll see you there. But you've got to promise to be enthusiastic when you meet me. Remember what I said about how you should act when I call? Well, that's what I want you to be like when we meet as well—happy, enthusiastic, ecstatic. Does that sound like a plan?"

"Okay, you got it."

"Cool. See you then."

Once I've worked out the arrangements, I get the hell off the phone! There's no reason to linger on now that the next step has been agreed upon, and a phone call over five minutes is too long anyway. I always strive to make it sweet and simple. I save my energy for what counts: the mini-date.

STEP **62**

# The Nickname Tease

> I don't generally recommend gimmicks because
> they can trip you up, sound rehearsed, or make
> you lazy, but one gimmick you just gotta love
> is the nickname tease.

A woman's curiosity is a wonderful tool. Use it. All the time. Keep her guessing. Keep her intrigued. Drop little teases and hints that you have to follow up on later.

I don't recommend gimmicks because they can trip you up, sound rehearsed, or make you lazy, but one gimmick I love is the Nickname Tease. If the phone conversation is playful, I casually mention that I've thought of the best nickname for her, but I can't tell her what it is until we meet in person. Until then, I let her curiosity run wild.

Of course, I really do need to have a nickname for the girl. And it's got to be sweet, endearing, romantic, flattering, and at least vaguely related to something about her. Nicknames usually sound a bit silly to me and you may feel self-conscious using them at first, but women really eat this kind of thing up.

After a few months of practice, you'll be great at coming up with nicknames. Until then, use this simple formula; it always impresses, even if it sounds embarrassing coming out of your mouth.

1.  Think of something yummy (sugar, butter, chocolate) or something descriptive of food (sweet, spicy, creamy, hot). It seems crazy, I know, but food is sexy.

2.  Think of the one part of her appearance that stands out compared to other women, or even better, something about her appearance she clearly loves, and use one word to describe it.

3.  Put the two words together, and you've got a romantic, endearing, and sexy nickname: Sugar Lips, Spicy Thighs, Creamy Butt. All right, maybe not all combinations will work, but I'm sure you can come up with something.

Once we're together, I'm not in a rush to tell the girl my secret because (and yes, it works!) she might be willing to make out with me or end up in bed with me just to find out her nickname. Or I can bring it up to tease her when the conversation lags; it's the perfect fluff filler. Don't overuse it, though, twice should be enough.

Intrigue is a valuable tool, and the Nickname Tease is one of the best gimmicks for creating intrigue. If she's on the fence, it will push her to your side; if she's into you already, it will make her that much more eager to please you and it gives her a great excuse to do that (because some girls just need to find an excuse to justify having sex).

And for heaven's sake, once you tell her the secret, *always remember her nickname*. Nothing loses a girl faster than giving her something special just between the two of you, and then forgetting about it.

STEP **63**

# The Mini-Date

Don't get cocky and think you're home free just
because she's agreed to get coffee. There will still
be bumps in the road.

Look, let's get something straight right now: You are never, ever
going on a date with a woman you hardly know. That's for
chumps. There are a zillion better and cheaper ways to get to know
a woman than paying for an expensive dinner at a fancy restaurant. Neither will you be able to impress her by taking her to
McDonald's, in case you think you'll still be offering her a romantic dinner experience while saving some money. Play sports
or exercise together, rent a movie, meet for a cup of coffee. Get
that whole "Can I ask you for a date" mentality out of your
mind, because you're never going to:

1. Take her somewhere. You're going together.
2. Pay for her food and drinks. Unless it's something really
   small (a cup of tea, for example) and you *want* to make a
   friendly gesture, she pays for herself. It's called going
   dutch. If she has a problem with that, then she's not the
   girl for you.

3.  Feel pressured to entertain her. By this point, she should
    be the one feeling pressured to entertain you. If you're
    ever going to be successful with women, you have to
    make her want you more than you want her—or at least
    make her believe that's what's happening.

Don't get cocky and think you're home free just because she's
agreed to get coffee. There will still be bumps in the road. She
made a spontaneous decision to meet when she was feeling really
attached to you, and now she's had time away to think about it.
Don't expect things to go smoothly; you'll just find yourself disappointed when she doesn't agree to jump straight into bed.
There's still work to be done, but that's half the fun.

Okay, okay, it's ten percent of the fun, but only because sex
with a woman you desire is some of the best, if not *the* best fun
you can have in life. You'll have to embrace and enjoy the whole
process, otherwise you'll have a hard time getting to Step Sixty-
nine.

I always try to convince girls to meet me at a coffeehouse I
know a few blocks from my apartment. It's within walking distance, so it's convenient for inviting her home, and we can have
a short romantic walk (past two fast-food restaurants and a gas
station, but who's really going to notice?) on the way back.

But before I get to that point, I follow some very simple
rules:

1.  I always arrive early and wait outside for her to arrive.

2.  When I see her, I act enthusiastic. Hopefully, she will
    act enthusiastic when she sees me, not only because
    she's excited about meeting me but because I told her
    to be enthusiastic when I asked for her number and
    then reinforced that suggestion in the follow-up phone
    call.

3. I immediately give her a big hug. Then I take her hand and hold it all the way to the counter. It's a great way to get kino started.

4. I say to her at the counter, "I assume we're going dutch." She may look surprised, but she'll agree. I order, wait for her to order, then lead her to the table by the hand.

5. The whole time, of course, I'm watching her reaction and playing off her cues. She is naturally going to be nervous about meeting me, but if I lead her with my actions I should see her go from nervous to happy, smiling, starry-eyed, and glowing within a space of a few minutes.

Once we start talking, it's no different than meeting a stranger in a bar. I will be eliciting values, becoming the man of her dreams, getting kino, moving into sexual talk, and Kiss Close once again. But this time I'm going to be direct, enthusiastic, and energetic. The mini-date is not the time for subtlety. Enthusiasm is contagious, so I use it.

One of the best moves you can use on a mini-date is the foot flirt. It's innocent, it's private, and it's something she can return without fear of social reprisal. So after a minute, I touch her feet twice with my feet and see how she responds. I don't stomp; I just rub my foot along hers and leave it there. And, of course, I always sync this kino with something positive in the conversation.

If her response is ambiguous—in other words, she isn't rubbing my ankle but she isn't pulling away either—I touch her again and say, "Are you foot flirting with me?" in a joking way. Then I touch her again. If she starts to respond, I know I'm in.

# STEP **64**

# The Kiss Invitation

Simply put, after a kiss invitation, you are with a girl who knows what to expect. The reason you are inviting her to your house, which you do while gazing into her eyes after coming out of a kiss, is perfectly clear. No surprises.

We've had a great meeting. I've kept it short and to the point, and now it's time to move on to a romantic place to continue what we've started. The goal here is . . . well, you have to decide what your ultimate goal is, but if all you end up doing is having a great conversation and becoming friends with her, then you've just wasted a bunch of my time, your time, and quite frankly, her time as well because at this point she is very much considering the possibility of having sex with you. At this point she is simply waiting for you to make all the right moves and none of the wrong ones, but if you stall, believe me, she's gonna be even more disappointed than you.

But how can you know for sure that sex is on her mind as well? A woman's mind (if not everything else) is impenetrable, right? Of course not. This whole seduction is built on making her think what you want her to think and watching her reaction to make sure she's thinking right.

Did that sound complicated? Then let me make it simple: You've got to make sure she understands why she's coming to your house before you extend the invitation.

It doesn't matter how you say it. Sometimes I just throw bull-shit to the wind and say, "Let's go to my place."

Sometimes I go silly: "Come over to my place and check out my Chia pet."

Sometimes I work it into the conversation. She likes hip hop? Then she should come over and see my collection. She likes cool furniture? Hey, I've got furniture at my place!

It's not the talking that matters, it's the action. Within three seconds of meeting her, I'm holding her hand. Within three min-utes, I'm foot flirting. Whenever she responds, I get more inti-mate: I stroke her hand, touch her hair, slide over to her side of the table (I love booths!) and hold her waist.

Finally, I try the ultimate test: a kiss. *Do not skip the kiss.* The kiss is essential for two reasons.

1. Kissing is the ultimate test of her intentions. Kissing is a huge decision for a girl, so be sure she's ready to make that leap now because, in order to sleep with you, she's going to have to make a decision on your worthiness at some point. Better to have her make it earlier in the evening, when she's comfortable, and have it be some-thing that on the surface seems as "innocent" as a kiss. If she's reluctant to kiss you, she'll be reluctant to do any-thing more when she comes back to your place. Don't even think of inviting her home until she kisses you con-vincingly.

2. Kissing is a powerful aphrodisiac. She may have been thinking of coming and checking out your Chia pet any-way, but now when she does it, she's horny. Kiss her long

enough, and she's liable to invite herself over—with less-than-pure intentions already in mind.

Simply put, after a Kiss Invitation, you are with a girl who knows what to expect. The reason you are inviting her to your house, which you do while gazing into her eyes after coming out of the kiss, is perfectly clear. No surprises. When she accepts the invitation, she knows what it means. And that's all because of the kiss.

So remember, it's not the invitation that matters, it's the timing. If you're going to invite a girl home with you—and there's no point in reading this book if that's not your intention—then you'd better kiss-test and get her excited first.

---

### The Quickie

Of course, there's always a second option, or even a third. Some players are adamantly against even trying to invite the woman over to your place. Why risk having her slip out of the mood on the drive home?

This is a valid point. It can happen sometimes. Personally I think inviting her home is the classy way to go and should always be your first option, even with the additional risk. If she doesn't want to wait for sex at your place, by all means fulfill her every fantasy, but only take this route if she indicates it first.

Some guys, however, don't want to stop with horny. They like to get a woman so riled up she's ready to find a secluded spot—the alley, a doorway, the parking lot, the bathroom of the coffee shop—and get straight to it.

Well, what can I say? If it works, it works. But you'd better be certain that's her goal before you go groping her in the back of your Volkswagen.

STEP **6 5**

# The Dinner Invite

> By forcing the situation, I made her realize she
> wanted to get to know me better. And, even more
> important, she now realizes that she's more into
> me than I am into her. Now she thinks she's
> chasing me, which is exactly where I want her.

What happens if she doesn't want to kiss and kino over coffee?
Don't worry, that's perfectly understandable. Let's think about
the situation. I am in a public place with this girl, a few blocks
from her office. She has a boyfriend. She might be thinking, *I'd
love to, but what if someone sees me? I don't really even know this guy
that well yet!*

So she keeps it on the level. We're having a good conversation—a little cold at first, but she's warming up, starting to laugh
and open up her posture—but she isn't responding to the foot
flirt. What to do, what to do?

One option is to cut this meeting off right now, in which case
I say I'm busy and have to go, making it obvious that she hasn't
lived up to my expectations. She'll either be relieved—this isn't
really her style, and she's not about to change for me—or she'll
start to chase. She's been cold, sure, but she didn't mean to

throw away this wonderful opportunity. The look on her face will tell me immediately whether she really wanted to take this encounter any further or not.

The brush-off is best for really gorgeous women. They expect you to fawn over them, so when you turn the tables and blow them off, they get confused . . . and intrigued. It also works very well if she's being a total bitch. If she thinks she has enough power to play you like that, you either have to turn the tables on her or bail. There's no third way. It's that simple.

But that's not the case here. This girl is cute, though not a perfect ten. And she's not being cold, just wary. So I take a slightly different approach: the blow off plus dinner invite (essentially extending an invitation as I leave, one of the most effective hooks).

I give her one last foot flirt, but she moves out of the way, so right away I say, "Look, I've got to go. It was very nice meeting you (lean in, touch her hand or the anchor on her elbow). It was fun."

I stand up and begin to put my jacket on. She looks surprised. She starts to say something, then stops and looks away.

Perfect. Even she wasn't sure she wanted this to go any further. By forcing the situation, I made her realize she wanted to get to know me better. And, even more important, she now realizes she's more into me than I am into her. Now she thinks she's chasing me, which is exactly where I want her.

But I'm not going to let this slip away by leaving it totally in her court to invite herself over. I've already won; why risk it? I give her about thirty seconds while I throw away my coffee cup, get my jacket ready, etc. If she doesn't bite, I say:

"But how about dinner at my place?"

She looks up. "What?"

"Come over to my place for dinner. Tomorrow night. At seven."

"Tomorrow? I can't."

"Okay then, I'll see you." At this point, I'm ready to walk away. She needs to chase me a little here, or this is just going to be a struggle the whole way. Very rarely will the girl just leave it at "so long." Ninety-five percent of the time, if I've calibrated her even close to correctly, the reason she can't come is because she's actually busy or playing a little game with you of looking busy. If that's the case, she's going to summon up enough inner strength (even if she's painfully shy and inexperienced) to suggest an alternative.

"How about Friday?"

I think about it for a second. "I can't on Friday (knowing that you're free Friday evening right off the bat is not very good), but Sunday I'll be free."

She smiles. "It's a date!"

"It's a dinner. So come hungry."

STEP **66**

# Dinner at Home

I hear you, I hear you. You don't want to actually have to spend time or effort cooking. Don't worry, neither do I. I hate cooking. Which is why I'm so happy that prepared food that looks home-made is available at most grocery stores these days. I usually go with a pre-roasted chicken that I can just throw in the oven, a salad in a bag, and a freshly made chocolate cake. I'm not a big chocolate fan myself, but women seem to love it. I also buy three or four small chocolate-covered strawberries, which I'll mention in a minute.

If she asks if it's homemade, I tell her the truth: I got it pre-cooked from the grocery. The point isn't to impress her with the food and make her think I'm a good cook; it's to get her to my place so I can elicit values, sex talk, and kino the hell out of her away from prying eyes.

There are numerous benefits to the meal at home beyond the fact that it's far cheaper and less supplicating than buying her dinner at a restaurant.*

*As I've said before, never buy a woman dinner at a restaurant unless you consider her your one and only girlfriend, and the relationship is serious. And then only buy if she's shown you she is willing to buy you things in other situations. You don't want to ever be in a relationship (short of marriage, but that's a whole different story) where you're *expected* to support a woman financially.

1. I make the meal romantic with candles, music, and mood lighting.

2. Food is a sensual pleasure (oral gratification) and when I feed a woman she associates that sensual feeling with me, especially since I'm reinforcing that idea with verbal and physical anchors.

3. I can literally feed her, making the pleasure that much greater. Remember the chocolate.covered strawberries?

4. By making something for her, I've given myself an air of competence and self-assurance. I've cared and provided for her without supplicating, which makes even the most uptight women feel more comfortable, relaxed, and, yes, uninhibited.

Never forget why you brought her over: to get her comfortable, sexually excited, and ready to end the evening the right way—the horizontal way (unless, of course, you prefer to experiment with some of the more exotic positions). Remember, never extend the invitation to the bedroom or start to undress her until you've nailed the Kiss Close. That kiss is the golden invitation to the dance.

STEP **67**

# Eliminate the Final Blocker

After a heavy make-out session, some women will throw up one final blocker. Why? Because there is no doubt that you are expecting to be in flagrante delicto tonight. She wants it—you can't just walk away from heavy petting—but for whatever reason (morals, societal pressure, guilt about the boyfriend) many women make one last attempt to resist.

Which, of course, this girl does. Not surprising. She's clearly a good girl who is inexperienced with this kind of encounter. No matter what type of girl she is, though, there are only four types of objections at this point. It's my job to determine exactly what her objection is and to counter it.

## Objection #1: She really doesn't want to have sex.

I can't stress this enough: if she really doesn't want to have sex, *do not force the issue*. That is her prerogative. It's your job to get her so hot and bothered *she can't resist*; if you've failed to do that, then let her be. Once she says no, you stop. Period. Even if you're convinced she wants what you've got, never force yourself on a woman.

That having been said, anything short of a "no" (like "I don't know") still leaves room for negotiation.

## Objection #2: She's got moral issues.

Many women want to have sex, but when it comes time to perform they hesitate for societal or moral reasons (she doesn't want to seem like a tramp, she's worried about diseases, her religion is against it, etc.). Once you know her specific objection, use the fake female friend to turn her mindset around.

If, for instance, she doesn't want to be slutty (in her own mind) tell her: "I just talked to my friend Lucy about this, and she says it is so unbelievably unfair that men can make love to any woman they choose, but if a woman wants to express her sexual liberty, she is frowned upon. I completely agree with her."

If there's something holding her back, but you can't find out what it is through eliciting values (sometimes it's buried pretty deep!), try this gimmick: "Imagine I have a magic wand and I can use it to make anything you wish disappear. Just tell me one thing you'd like me to make disappear in order for you to feel comfortable, because I hate to see you missing out on things you should enjoy. It can be anything—a person, an attitude of our society, something about yourself, something about me—absolutely anything. Now what would that one thing be?"

## Objection #3: She's just not sure.

If she's just "not sure" about going all the way, tell her that you understand and agree with her concerns, but you just can't help thinking about what a great time the two of you would have. Even act like you agree with her: "We shouldn't do it, and when we do we shouldn't enjoy it so much. And please don't try to convince me that you really want to do it . . ."

What she's really looking for is a Mental Escape Hatch: an "excuse" to justify going all the way with a virtual stranger. It could be the wine, the music, the romance in the air . . . it doesn't matter. All you're trying to do is throw out excuses (More wine? Do you like this music?) until she latches onto one for herself.

Take a step back. Say you understand (even if you don't, it doesn't matter). Take a break from her by disappearing into the kitchen or bathroom for a few minutes, or engrossing yourself with the newspapers, or checking for new e-mail for a few moments. Make sure she has nothing else to do (if she starts watching TV or calls her friend, this won't work). Then in a few minutes when you turn back to her and contnue almost from where you left off, first by talking, then some light kino, etc., you'll be sure to progress further than before. But never force it; respect it. If she blocks again at some point, repeat the process and she'll come around eventually.

## Objection #4: She's got a personal hang-up.

Many women have hang-ups about being with a man, usually centered around one of three things: 1. they feel inadequate sexually, usually due to inexperience; or 2. they feel unclean, especially down there, and want to clean up first; or 3. they are uncomfortable being naked with a man and having him see their body. Yes, even the gorgeous ones. Society is really pressuring these women on how they look and society's a bitch.

Always be sensitive to her hesitancy. If she wants to do it with the lights off, do it with the lights off. If she wants to go to the bathroom first, let her go. If she hesitates to ask, just tell her, "Hey, why don't you go freshen up in the bathroom while I get out the champange and the cake, so that you'll feel fresh for the dessert." Like I said, most people like to be told what to do and why. Once she's in the bathroom, she'll be sure to freshen up *everywhere*, just in case . . .

In this scenario, it soon becomes clear through eliciting values that she's . . . yes, a virgin! That's a double-edged sword. She's waited so long that she wants the first time to be special, but she's also embarrassed because she's never been with a man before and doesn't know what to do.

I play off both these objections by taking the lead and really talking her through the experience. I tell her not only what to do (at first "just relax" but later more complicated things), but what I'm doing and why. That way, I take the pressure off her to perform and at the same time assure her that I'm an expert who's going to make her first time very, very special.

STEP **68**

# Sex Tonight

**Enjoy the ride.**

Sorry, fellas, this isn't a sex manual. For the next hour (at least), you're on your own. But I can give you one important piece of advice that will never fail you: Pay attention to her. If she gets hers, you'll get yours, so always make her your first priority. Watch her reaction. Figure out what she likes and doesn't like. As John Cleese said in *The Meaning of Life*: Don't stampede for the clitoris. Let her tell you when she wants to go all the way— and don't be afraid to make her beg for it a few times.

Don't worry, newbies, it's not as hard as you think. If you do something wrong, most women will tell you about it and tell you how to do it right. So take direction if you're new or take charge if you're experienced. Above all, make sure you do her good and not only will she want to come again, don't be surprised if some of her girlfriends suddenly start to flirt with you as well. Girls like to brag and since a good guy is always hard to find, they hardly ever waste an opportunity to tell their girlfriends how good their guy is in bed if he really is. On the other hand, if the guy is lousy, sooner or later that'll get around as well, so make sure your reputation is going to be top notch.

Should you require more tips and tricks for various situations, an already huge but still growing source can be found on my original website at www.layguide.com. But for now, this book should get you at least started if this is all new to you, or keep you on track if you want to polish up your game, so I hope you've enjoyed the ride.

# STEP **69**

# Enjoy Every Second

That's why the guys in the know don't call
seduction The Work or The Race. They call it
The Game.

What? You're still here? I thought you were ... oh, never mind.

Well, I did promise 69 steps, so if I don't give you one more, you're going to be disappointed, right? Yes, the previous 68 steps teach you everything you need to know, and your life is going to improve because of them, and you're going to see your greatest wish come true, but that doesn't matter, does it? I promised 69, and if you only get 68, you're going to be disappointed.

That's a valuable lesson: always deliver on your promises. Or even better, don't make promises. Never say, "Baby, I'm going to rock your world with the greatest night of your life." She should be making that promise to you.

And one more thing, my friends. Always remember that life isn't about the destination; it's about the journey. If you measure your success by the boots that get knocked, you're just putting pressure on yourself, and that makes it harder to succeed.

To be a true success, you not only have to follow the 69 steps in this book, you have to *enjoy* them. All of them. Every single one. And believe me, once your mind is right, you will. You'll turn the awkward, scary art of seduction into the most pleasurable experience of your life.

Really.